S0-BDS-628

# NOTRE DAME REVIEW

# NOTRE DAME REVIEW

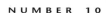

NUMBER 10

*Editors*
John Matthias
William O'Rourke

*Senior Editor*     Steve Tomasula
*Founding Editor*     Valerie Sayers

*Managing Editor*
Marie Munro

*Contributing Editors*
Matthew Benedict
Gerald Bruns
Seamus Deane
Stephen Fredman
Sonia Gernes
Jere Odell
Kymberly Taylor Haywood
James Walton
Henry Weinfield

*Editorial Assistants*
Anne Bracewell
Stacy Cartledge
John Crawford
Douglas Curran
Shannon Doyne
Robert Imbur
Marinella Macree
David Alyn Mayer
Nonieqa Goddess Ramos
Amy Reese
Blake Sanz
Laura Schafer
Mike Smith
Josie Vodicka

The *Notre Dame Review* is published semi-annually. Subscriptions: $15(individuals) or $20 (institutions) per year or $250 (sustainers). Single Copy price: $8. Distributed by Media Solutions, Huntsville, Alabama; Ingram Periodicals, LaVergne, Tennesse; and International Periodical Distributors, Solana Beach, California. We welcome manuscripts, which are accepted from September through April. Please include a SASE for return. Please send all subscription and editorial correspondence to: *Notre Dame Review*, The Creative Writing Program, Department of English, University of Notre Dame, Notre Dame, IN 46556.
The *Notre Dame Review* is indexed in *The American Humanities Index*.
*Notre Dame Review* copyright 2000 by the University of Notre Dame
ISSN: 1082-1864
*Body & Soul* ISBN 1-892492-09-1
Cover Art: Eduardo Kac, *Genesis*, 1998-1999, *E.coli* bacteria genetically engineered to carry the text "Let man have dominion over the fish of the sea and over the fowl of the air and over every living thing that moves upon the earth." Photo courtesy of Julia Friedman & Associates, Chicago.

# Contents

# BODY & SOUL

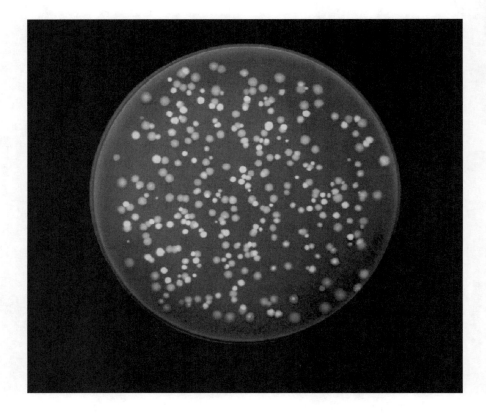

*Genesis*, shown here and on the front cover, is an installation by artist Eduardo Kac originally mounted at the O.K. Center for Contemporary Art, Linz, Austria. At its heart is a petri dish of *E. Coli* bacteria, genetically altered to carry an excerpt from the Biblical book of Genesis: "Let man have dominion over the fish and the sea and the fowl of the air and over every living thing that moves upon the earth." An ultraviolet light directed at the bacteria could be activated by viewers using the Internet, thus accelerating the natural rate of mutation of both the bacteria and the message it contained.

Photo courtesy of Julia Friedman & Associates, Chicago.

# CAEDMON'S HYMN

*Translated by Paul Muldoon*

Now we must praise to the skies     the Keeper of the heavenly kingdom,
The might of the Measurer,     all he has in mind,
The work of the Father of Glory,     of all manner of marvel,


Our eternal Master,     the main mover.
It was he who first summoned up,     on our behalf,
Heaven as a roof,     the holy Maker.


Then this middle-earth,     the Watcher over humankind,
Our eternal Master,     would later assign
The precinct of men,     the Lord Almighty.

# FROM LANGLAND'S PIERS PLOWMAN: GLUTTONY

*Translated by Ken Smith*

Now begins Glutton to come to confession
and moves towards the church, to confess his guilt.
Fasting on a Friday he went forth
by the house of Betty the brewer, who bade him good morning,
and where was he going the brew-wife asked him.
    'to Holy Church,' said he, 'to hear mass,
and then to sit and be shriven and sin no more.'
    'I have good ale, gossip Glutton, will you try it?'
    'Have you,' said he, 'any hot spices?'
    'I have pepper and peony and a pound of garlic,
a farthing-worth of fennel seeds I bought for fast days.'
    Then in goes Glutton with great oaths thereafter.
Sissy the shoemaker sat on the bench,
Wat the game-warden and his drunken wife,
Tim the tinker and two of his workmen,
Hick the hackney-man and Hugh the needler,
Clarice of Cock's Lane and the church clerk,
Sir Piers of Pridie and Purnel of Flanders,
a hayward, a hermit, the hangman of Tyburn,
Dave the ditcher, with a dozen dodgy characters
in the shape of porters and pick-purses and bald tooth-pullers,
a fiddler and a rat-catcher, a street-sweeper and his mate,
a rope-maker, a road-runner, and Rose the dish-seller,
Godfrey the garlic-monger and Griffith the Welshman,
and a heap of old clothes sellers, early in the morning
with good cheer gave Glutton good ale as a gift.
    Clement the cobbler threw off his cloak
and put it up for a game of 'New Fair.'
Hick the hackney-man put his hood in after
and asked Bit the butcher to be on his side.
Chapmen were chosen to appraise this prize,
that whoever had the hood should not have the cloak,
and that the better thing, by the arbiters, should compensate the worse.

They rose up rapidly and whispered together
and appraised these pennyworths apart by themselves,
and there were oaths stacked high, for one would get the worse.
They could not in conscience accord truthfully
till they asked Robin the rope-maker to arise
and named him umpire, that there be no argument.
      Hick the hostler had the cloak,
on condition that Clement should fill the cup,
and have Hick's hood and look happy;
and whoever first took it back should rise right away
and greet sir Glutton with a gallon of ale.
      There was laughing and louring and 'let go the cup!'
bargains and beverages began to start,
and they sat so till evensong, and sang now and again,
till Glutton had gobbled a gallon and a gill.
His guts began to grumble like two greedy sows;
he pissed a half-gallon in *pater-noster* time,
he blew his round horn at his ridge-bone's end,
so all who heard that horn held their noses after
and wished it well scoured with a wisp of briars.
He could neither step nor stand without a staff,
and then he began to go like a minstrel's bitch
sometimes sideways and sometimes backwards,
like someone laying lines to trap birds.
      And when he got to the door, then his eyes dimmed,
and he stumbled at the threshold and fell to the earth,
and Clement the cobbler caught him by the waist
and to lift him aloft laid him on his knees.
But Glutton was a big boor and troubled in the lifting
and coughed up a mess in Clement's lap;
there's no hound so hungry in Hertfordshire
dares lap up that leaving, so unlovely it smelt.
      With all the woe of this world his wife and his daughter
bore him to his bed and got him therein,
and after all this excess he had a bout of torpor;
he slept Saturday and Sunday till sunset.
Then he woke wan and would have a drink;
The first word he spoke was 'Who's got the bowl?'
His wife and his conscience reproached him for his sin;
he grew ashamed, that scoundrel, and confessed himself swiftly

to Repentance like thus: 'Have pity on me,' he said,
'Lord who art aloft and shapes all that lives.
    To you, god, I, Glutton, admit myself guilty
in that I have trespassed with my tongue, I can't say how often,
sworn 'God's soul and his sides!' and 'So help me, God Almighty!'
there was never need so many times falsely;
and overate at supper and sometimes at noon
more than my system could take.
And like a dog that eats grass I began to throw up
and spilled what I might have saved—I cannot speak for shame
the villainy of my foul mouth and my foul maw—
and fast-days before noon I fed myself ale
beyond reason, among dirty jokers to hear their dirty jokes.
    For this, good God, grant me forgiveness
for all my worthless life for all my life-time,
for I swear to very God, despite any hunger or thirst,
fish shall never on a Friday digest in my stomach
till my aunt Abstinence has given me leave—
and yet have I hated her all my lifetime.'

# TOLSTOI: A DAY IN THE LIFE

*Michael B. McMahon*

The tsar of Russian letters,
dressed in clogs he's made of bark
and a peasant blouse
of the coarsest hemp, quits
the den at Yasnaya Polyana,
joins his family for lunch.

The writing's gone well—
a tract on the evils of meat
and sex, notes for another
urging us to scorn
worldly goods. *Go live
among the poor and serve
their crushing needs. Anything
less is spiritual sloth.*

His dining room shimmers
with sunlight and Brahms.
Sergey, the second of thirteen
children, sits at the grand, regaling
guests with *Hungarian Dances.*
Applause at the final chord, smiles
and nods from live-in tutors,
house physicians, artists
from Paris, family friends. Fatigued
by butchering chores—
three chickens, a lamb and forty
pounds of beef to fortify the soup—
three of the servants
bustle about with silver tureens.

Leo Nikolaevich, in stately
command of his great white beard,
fixes one with piercing eyes,
waves off the soup. He'll dine
again on a crust of bread,
a cup of Russian tea.

## *FROM* POEMS IN MEMORY OF TED HUGHES

*Daniel Weissbort*

### DEPARTURE OF THE HEARSE

No darkness under a stone.
Just light, an end.
And after that, endlessness,
unmoving, of an engine stopped.

The crows, after your funeral, drawn upwards,
as we stood in the rain
and waited for the hearse to leave
with the body we'd known you by?

### AN EXAGGERATION

You'd take me fishing with you—
I brought you luck, you said.
You'd search the bank for the right spot.
When I'd recaptured your attention,
I'd look for topics to reward you.
Much or most you'd let go by,
but then I'd hit on something.
I'd bang around while you watched
rather absently, reflectively,
your mind more on the river.
And then your voice would come,
oceanic really, joining continents
from which my separated selves
hailed one another.

## UNTRANSLATED

I stand in his workroom, stand—
the window frames his view—
trees, bushes, the church steeple—
green, green, green,
and the church steeple.

He was fixing a translation of *Sir Gawain*—
The Middle English text and several versions in front of him.
But didn't make a beeline for the alliteration.
But does that surprise me?
I want to ask him, wondering:

…and Aeschylus, *The Oresteia*—
the *Icelandic Sagas*, an attempt at an appreciation—
did you have in mind to embrace all this?
And still more—
There was *Gilgamesh*, for instance,
plans for a stage version?

. . .

But, in these pages of mine, there is no you to ask.
Do I keep you alive for me by not transcribing you,
not finding a form of words for you—
the look of you and your look?
Do I keep you in the original,
untranslated?

# HARTLAND, NORTH DEVON

I went there several times,
but only once or twice with you.
Remember the view, of course,
the world wrought large.
But better, our lying on that shingle beach,
you lobbing stones into the waters.

No more.  What we talked of,
your words, all gone.
Only the gesture, thoughtful,
propped on an elbow,
eyes narrowed in the wind,
nibbling something, a blade of grass.
Lobbing stones.

A small, almost cozy yet battleship-grey cove,
the waters unagitated—
air with gulls—
a few clouds, not a sunny day.
Not as though we had fallen from on high,
but as though there were no call on us,
or we were playing truant,
idly on a beach of stones.

There was an intimacy, a breathlessness, up close—
the great cliffs, banished, distant,
as in a painting of them
in some provincial gallery.

# EL DESDICHADO

*After Nerval*

*Michael Perkins*


I am anthracite, pitch-dark but shiny,
Like the spot under the devil's tail.
Scorpions are my hook-tailed familiars.

Where I go I scream my curses into song;
I play on Orpheus's lyre Eurydice's lament.

In the shadow of inglorious deeds I lurk,
Unlucky, unfortunate, good for nothing,
The hermit of the blind alley, the saint of wrong;
The light of my life has gone out.


*In memory of William Bronk, 1917-1999*

# SMALL COURTESIES

*by R. M. Kinder*

The Fan-T-Sci conference descended on the Delmar Hotel on a Friday afternoon in November. The Missouri sky was already shading toward its winter gray, moist, and low, but shimmering, as if a colder layer moved above. Inside the hotel, the employees, though all decent people, were tired and harried, and felt disconcerted by the nature of the guests. The clerks tried not to stare, but they covertly assessed the arriving group. The night supervisor called the manager, and moments later was instructed to provide extra security for the duration of this conference. Costs would escalate, but possibly food and drink sales would more than compensate. Hotel security contacted the police station and requested five of the city's finest for an off-duty job at good pay. Just in case.

Truly, this was no common conference. A new world mingled in the lobby, then dispersed in singles or small groups toward the stairs, elevator, or bar. One woman was dressed in silver sequins that clung to her torso and limbs as if they actually grew there. Only her face and her pale hands—the latter with silver nails at least three inches long—indicated that flesh lay beneath the sequins. She rippled when she moved, a most mesmerizing sight for everyone in the lobby. She noticed the attention and laughed. The sound brought chills to one clerk, and glances among them all. Another female wore flowing red chiffon—with nothing underneath but billowing body. Huge and rolling, she registered using her own pen, and the red ink name sworled violently. Most of the women were in black; most were buxom; all were on display. Male gazes could move from breasts that peeked, perked, to those that swung or hung pendant like sinking moons. The men seemed less colorful, but more ominous overall. Only a few were proportioned or attractive, and they highlighted their best features: A young man with the body of a dancer wore tight briefs, from which narrow silk bands led down his legs and over his upper body, creating the illusion of shirt and slacks; another wore form-fitting silver, no sequins, but with the sides missing, the front and back laced together. Most of the males, though, were misshapen, too tall, or too thin, obese, squat, or perhaps with skinny legs beneath a pear body, or narrow shoulders above a globe of rump. A cadaverish man in black leather had somehow shaped his long orange hair into spikes, so no one could stand near him. Beneath the jutting front spikes, his eyes appeared like black holes. His teeth were orange or had been painted so.

A gnomish man in green velvet looked up at the doorman and said in a low, soft voice, "We're not freaks. During the year we're just normal people with normal jobs. This is our holiday. Our chance to be different."

The doorman, who had a nice home in the suburbs and two children in college, didn't understand why this guy was explaining to him. He didn't know whether to feel threatened, because maybe the dwarf was flirting, or complimented, because he looked like a man one should explain to. "Well," he said, "we all need a vacation from time to time."

"We won't be causing any trouble or anything."

"Well, that's good. You might tell the manager that."

"We will. We're always good guests."

Behind the desk, a nightclerk mumbled, "We're in for something different this weekend," and read a few names to his coworker. "Dala Coflera, Zi Ki Lai, Larry Lech, Mylaika Rakon." He scrolled down the computer list. "Hey, a John Brown. Probably a spy." He was pleased with himself and had managed to pass from trepidation to anticipation. Usually he was bored at work. "Let it rain, let it pour," he said, sat on the high stool by the desk, and watched what was shaping up.

One of the night staff told the supervisor she needed to go home. Her babysitter had just called and her son was ill. "My God," she said to herself, hurrying across the filling parking lot, "it's like hell opened up." She was afraid of her own imagination and what such guests could induce in her. Even in the car, she felt unsafe, as if something horrible would pop up over the back seat and speak to her. When she got home, she asked the babysitter to stay for a while, but the girl couldn't. The woman and her son watched a comedy on television. The frantic, crazy humor made her tremble.

Meanwhile, on a one-way road from a small university miles away, a midwestern couple who had been dating only a month or so, and were already struggling for conversation or a tinge of passion, drove toward the conference. Their headlights turned the heavy mist into sparkle, but they couldn't see much beyond the light, just black shapes that must be a house, or barn, or closed country store.

"Where do people in this country go?" she said. "The houses are always dark even early in the evening, like people are already in bed. Sometimes it's like the world has died and I'm coasting alone."

"People save electricity. If you look close, there's probably a light toward the back of the house."

"I leave every light on when I'm home, and some when I'm not."

"I've noticed."

She didn't like that statement, and he knew it. Both understood the implication, that he found her wasteful with money. He was a saver, a healthy man who worked out daily, read much, and had a strong sex drive. She was older, thin, chainsmoked, loved fat and chocolate, read much, and also had a strong sex drive. Both were headstrong and lonely. She liked houses that were warm, that glowed at night like invitation to life, and she resented this bleak moist country of homegrown tightwads and tiny spirits. "I think," she said, "a house should look warm and inviting."

"Yours does, that's for sure. It's a nice effect." He meant that. Although he would never waste electricity in his own home, driving up to hers always made him feel the lights were for him especially. He thought perhaps she had a generous spirit and he hoped he did, too. "I'm always comfortable at your place," he said.

The moment was saved and they settled back into their new lovers' closeness.

She was the one who had received notice of the conference. It was in her mailbox at work, with "FYI, Keith," signed at the bottom. Keith was a fellow professor from another department, who sometimes smoked outside with her, where they talked of writing and individuality. When she told him she might attend the conference, he said, "Good, but let me warn you that it's not traditional, not academic like you're accustomed to. These people are into science fiction and fantasy. I think you're pretty liberal and will enjoy yourself. I know you're bored with the normal routine here."

That she was. But, being also wary of new things alone, she had invited along her friend, the thick-set man who had recently proven they were compatible in bed.

Now, she worried. "What if we don't like it? I'd hate to cost you time and money for a bad weekend."

"At the worst, we can stay in our room for two days." He took her hand and placed it on his thigh, then patted it. "You worry too much."

They felt very comfortable the rest of the drive, very much together and ready to risk a step into the unknown.

One wing of the hotel had been reserved for the Fan-T-Sci guests, but other guests were certainly aware of them and grouped closer together when entering the dining room or bar. A few ventured into the special wing and read the legend of events posted in that registration room. It seemed bland enough, listing introduction, icebreaker, awards, dance; for Saturday, readings, mixers, games, stage play, special sessions. One brave brown-suited man managed to swipe a fuller program from a table near the bar, guarded by a green-dressed gnome.

"Just checking it out," the guest explained. "Looks interesting."

The gnome seemed saddened. "Those programs are for members only. You don't look like one."

"I may be by morning," the guest laughed, and waved the program as he walked away. It made for good reading with his wife: "Listen to this. 'Condom prizes, Fleur-de-lis room 8:00; Cross-dance by Leonard the Lionhearted, 9:00. Saturday sessions: 10:00 Leather, Centurion Room; Metal, Skyline Room; Silk and Softer, Dahlia Room; Surprise, Charleston Ballroom.' God," the man said, "I'd like to go."

"They'd kill you for smirking."

"Probably." But he wondered if he could somehow dress to pass, just sneak in for one session. He wanted to see this other life.

The policemen, having conferred with the night supervisor, stationed themselves discreetly apart, covering elevators and exits. One had a full view of the rear parking lot, where lights were dimmer, especially in the heavily descending fog, and anyone dressed in black would be indiscernible. That policeman would occasionally have a smoke while he strolled the lot and sensed anything inappropriate. He was told by a green gnome, who startled him by appearing silently and suddenly at his side, that, "We're just ordinary people, you know. We assume a role this one weekend of the year. I'm an accountant myself. We're a courteous group, overall. We don't tolerate poor behavior." The policeman found that little guy somewhat sinister, maybe because of the fog, maybe because he had a slight lisp, maybe because he was too damned ingratiating. Sort of a protests-too-much guy.

Having become lost in the city streets, where signs were in ridiculous positions, and two-way streets became suddenly one-way only, without any indication of the direction of the one way—north, east, south, or west—the midwestern couple arrived later than they planned. Both were slightly embarrassed that she had used a green garbage bag for a dress-carrier. He felt a little more worldly than her, because he would never have carried such a contraption into a nice hotel. He would have left it in the car and brought it in later, draped over his arm. She held it up so the bottom of her pink dress wouldn't touch the carpet. It seemed to him like a flag of mediocrity, perhaps low-class. She, however, quickly decided that it was a sign of her true individuality, since the really wealthy, the really secure, broke all the damned rules. Only the middle class worried about correctness and they were the ones who made the world truly monotonous, because they were cowards. He signed them in, registering by two names but for one room, because, what-the-hey, they were what they were. Unmarried and together. Modern enough to be blunt about it. He steered her toward the elevator. "We couldn't get in the reserved wing. It's all filled up. Might be best anyhow, to be separate from the main group since we're not really fantasy writers."

"I am. One of my published pieces is a fantasy."

"Okay. But we still can't get in that wing. The clerk said the introduction has already started. We can drop our things off and get right over there." He carried the suitcases and thought briefly about liberated women. She hadn't offered to carry her own suitcase.

A cop by the elevator said, "Good to see you folks. Thought there weren't any normal people left in the city." He had a goodhearted laugh that brought crinkles around blue eyes. He was too heavy for a policeman, but then, the woman thought, a good nature was a strong force. She sure liked that trait.

"I got a feeling," her lover said, "that we're not going to fit in."
"Why?"
"Didn't you hear the officer?"
"Maybe it's a young group."
"Maybe."

In their room he wanted to make love before they began the evening. The wide bed with the gold bedspread sank deliciously when he fell backward, and he wanted her to immediately be taken by the manliness he presented, lying on his back, hands behind his head, so his broad chest expanded even more. If she would just unfasten his belt, unzip his pants, without his having to say a word, she'd be the woman for him, but she was worrying aloud about whether to change clothing now or just get to the meeting. He reluctantly rose, and put his arms around her from behind, cupping her small breasts. "We could skip the first meeting," he whispered. "Why don't we shower together and then change? We can go for drinks afterwards and meet the crew."

"I want to see what's going on," she said. "We can make love later."
"Planning things ruins them."
"Spontaneity can ruin good plans."

So now neither could be truly happy with the evening. He had been postponed and devalued; she had been made selfish and staid. Both felt guilty and in risk of loneliness. Why didn't anything ever just work out right? They left dressed as they were, in search of the conference registration room.

And there, though all but one of the conferees had gone on to the introduction leaving one member to man the table, and though all the other tables bore the familiar paper cups, coffee urns, beer cans, and plastic glasses of conferences all over the world, the midwestern couple knew they were at the edge of a decision, because the one person left had orange spikes for hair, and eyes buried deep in shadows and sinking flesh.

She strode up to the table and her lover, though hesitant, followed, feeling that he might be enlisting—which he had avoided during the last war. He didn't like confrontations of any kind.

"We want to register for the conference," she said.

"I don't think so," the orange-head said. "Are you already members?"

"No. Do we have to be?"

"If you've ever been to one of our conferences, you are. If not, you can sign up. But you don't look as if you're into sci-fi."

She couldn't bear being told what she could and could not do, and the chagrin brought her connection to mind. "Keith Parmenter suggested I come. I write fantasy."

The dark holes seemed to shift to her partner.

"He's with me."

"I don't think either of you will be very comfortable."

"I want to register."

He allowed them to. He gave them blank lapel cards to fill out, and obviously read the names they wrote. "You better wear the cards all the time," he said, "so people will know you've paid to attend."

Her lover was amazed anew at her fortitude. For a few moments he felt that he traveled in her wake, which he didn't particularly like. He did like the sway of her hips, and the curl of her hair, and that stride that was nothing less than bold. He held the door open for her to enter the gathering room.

Actually, there was no silence when they entered, though both felt as if there were. And both felt the prickle that comes from unseen eyes, though each, if turning, could have seen all the eyes. No one missed the couple's entrance. The speaker, laughing, had a brief lapse of sound, then launched off into the grand introduction of the guest entertainer, none other than Leonard the Lionhearted.

The couple had to sit up front, near where they had entered, because the room was full, full, full, to standing creatures in the back, and they had seats only because a small man dressed in green carried forward two folding chairs. "Welcome," he said, and the couple felt warm toward him for a human gesture and a familiar word. They sat.

Now the speaker was joining the audience, and music rolled out from behind them, fast and rumbling, a rock boogie, and people clapped and hooted and squealed. The couple didn't turn, because whatever was coming, was coming their way. A man gyrated past them into the space before the podium. He bumped, high-stepped, turned, wiggled that bottom, flipped his wrists, manly wrists, with strong hands. He was tall, muscular, with wild black hair falling mid shoulder, and with a black beard heavy enough for two hands to get lost. His long legs were hairy, too, so very male and strong, but the feet were encased in black stiletto heels that never faltered in intricate turns and quick, cute little twists. His tight buttocks were covered by black lace stretching to a bodice top, above which his chest hair curled ludicrously or sensuously. His red-painted lips synched the boogie words and he wooed the crowd with winks and kisses, all to a boogie beat. Keith Parmenter. Leonard the Lionhearted. He stopped one moment in front of the couple, his hips and hands in rhythm, and capped each head with one of his hands for one beat, switched hands for another cap, then was bouncing off, swishing past, shaking that bodice top as though breasts might fall out. The couple now felt better. They had been touched and welcomed and were special guests, not outsiders. They were the anointed. When he danced back down the aisle, the couple applauded as loudly as anyone and even turned in their seats, surreptitiously skimming the crowd and meeting a few glances. Not all were cold.

They had to sit for another few minutes while awards were given to the conference planners. Black and orange condoms, blown slightly full, some with faces painted on the ends.

She wondered if she would be sickened by herself later, for having not walked out, for being pleased at the dancer's recognition. She hoped her lover didn't blame her for the coarseness of this meeting. He wasn't suited for this kind of thing. He was more conservative. A nice guy. Beside her, the lover thought by God he might not be happy, but he hadn't sunk this low. He was going back to the room and maybe back home. He had nothing in common with these crazy loons. Sick cries for attention. Losers all. Jesus. He didn't know what to make of her, sitting there so calm. But maybe she wasn't. Maybe they'd laugh and get the hell out of here together.

Keith, now dressed in a gold-mesh jumpsuit, was waiting for them by the door, and drew them aside. "I'm glad you came," he said. "I hope you're not shocked. I warned you."

"You did, but I didn't know what you meant. Now I do."

"And you're offended?"

"Maybe. I don't know. I've never seen anything like this. I tell you what, though, you were really good. I was fascinated. You can dance like crazy. I never knew that."

"I'd prefer no one at work know."

"I'm not going to say a word."

Keith glanced at her partner who shook his head. "Don't worry. This isn't the kind of thing I would talk about."

"You two," Keith said, "are a little noticeable. If you've got some more casual clothes, you'd feel less conspicuous."

"We both brought conference clothes," she said. "Will they kick us out?"

"Of course not. Just wear your name tags. And have fun." He patted her hand, while nodding at someone yards away, a lovely black girl whose body was painted the same array of colors as the chiffon scarves she wore, so that she looked like a wispy tropical bird or a blossom coming into being. He hurried to her and the couple watched this perfect match impossible anywhere else in the world they knew.

They went back to their room and made love with the lamps out, but the drapes open, so the window was all moon-filtered gray. He poised himself above her as if he were a bird and would swoop into her forever. That's how they both felt when he entered her, like they rode a fierce warm wind together. Then they lay side by side, sweating, tired, and each still charged as if the night wouldn't let them rest.

"You want to go home?" she asked.

"Was thinking about it."

"I'd like to see the dance. Just for a little while. Then we could go if you want. Or we could get a good night's sleep and leave in the morning. Or maybe shop a while."

He thought it odd that she could think of shopping. What was shopping, anyhow? His head wouldn't clear enough to get hold of that thought, or any thought equally common.

Across town, the nightstaff woman let her babysitter go home, and she checked on her little boy who hadn't been sick at all, but who wasn't sleeping easily now, maybe from popcorn and cookies so late at night. Maybe from her own tension. Certainly, she herself wasn't feeling well. Her breath was ragged, which meant she needed to calm herself or she'd start hyperventilating and get panicky. She hated her damned nervous nature, having to guard against her own tendencies. But she'd had sense enough to take off work. She'd be vomiting by now if she had stayed there. Crazy people scared her to death.

The back-lot cop had an intuition about which one would be the troublemaker. It was that creepy green runt. He was too damned friendly. The other cops said he'd talked to each of them, gave each the same line about being normal people all year and just acting out fantasies during this conference. What kind of fantasies? Maybe there'd be a murder from someone thinking he was goddamn jack-the-ripper. Heaven knows the women were dressing like they longed to be victims of something.

The silver-sequin lady had to take six pills before she could attend the dance, and apply fresh makeup. She was a mass of pain and sometimes nausea. Beneath the silver, surgery scars crisscrossed her abdomen. Her breasts were foam and she loathed them. But she loved the reflection of Mylaika Rakon. She could swim there, in that vision, because visions never took treatments, felt terror, never lied, never died. She was her own mantra.

The midwestern lover refused to dress any differently for the dance, and besides, he couldn't if he wanted to. The change he brought was dressier than what he had on. Well, she asked, would he attend with her if she was wearing only a slip? Because that's what she was going to do. She had a black, long, half-slip, and if she wore it pulled up over her breasts, wore black stockings, let her hair down and put on gobs of makeup, she'd fit right in.

"What about shoes?"

She solved that. She pulled houseslippers from her suitcase and waved them at him. Silver slip-ons, with elastic pulling them tight. "Will you go with me dressed like this?"

"Why not? We're never going to see any of these people again."

Now each felt superior to the other and were separate as they walked down the hall to the elevator. When they emerged, he avoided the cop's eyes by lighting a cigarette, and falling a little behind her. He was with her when she entered the elevator to the other wing.

"Ashamed of me, I see," she said. "You don't need to accompany me."

"Somebody better. You're acting strange."

"I'm the same woman you came with."

"Maybe, but you're not attracting the same kind of man."

She thought that was astute, that he was caring for her in his way. "I do feel ridiculous," she said. "I mean, this is obviously a slip. Maybe I should change back."

"You've done it, let's go. Or let's go home."

"You're right. I made the choice. But if you get the least bit uncomfortable," she said, "we'll leave."

"I can take it as long as you can." He put his hand on the small of her back to guide her down the hall. "Whatever you do, don't stare. You don't know these people."

The small ballroom had a fountain in the center, with a low wall on which some guests sat. Others danced on the square tiled floor. The music was haunting and frantic, metallic, like wind through huge flutes. Colored globes hung like moons across the room. The couple sat on the fountain wall. Near them, a tiny, fragile blonde, who held a posture so rigid she looked like a statue, spoke with a brown-draped monk. He turned to assess the couple. Moments later both left, followed by the others, and the midwestern couple were alone by the fountain.

"I never felt so naked," she said. "I'm having chills."

"It's the water. Did you know you forgot your name tag?"

"My God, I did."

Across the dance floor, the statue and monk had stopped by Keith Parmenter. Now he crossed to the couple, smiling slightly. "So you found something to wear after all."

"Is it okay? I feel foolish."

"No. You're trying to fit in. That's good. Why don't you dance? Show everyone you want to mingle, not just watch."

"So people *are* noticing us."

"Yes, but that doesn't matter. Relax. Dance. Laugh. Get acquainted with the members."

They did dance, because they were certainly no worse at it than most of the others, better in fact, except for Keith and his lovely flower, for whom the dancers applauded. The couple envied that grace, though when they considered the source of the appreciation, were glad enough to be just competent dancers. He wished she had not worn the slip, because the excitement flushed her neck and chest with a funny bluish-red color that made her look older and more worn, and because with no waistline in the slip, and with her tiny breasts, she was a slat woman, not feminine at all. He wanted to desire her, even if it were just protective, but he felt she was asking for ugly attention and that made her ugly. She felt terribly alone in his arms, because he had a way of withdrawing that she could sense, even when he denied it, so he was like a force against her. It was wearying. She couldn't bear the weight of his discontent. Her own was heavy enough.

Someone stopped them from dancing by touching each simultaneously. It was a small man, dressed in green velvet. His shoes were green, too, with curling tops.

"We have to ask you to leave," he said.

They were both taken aback, partly from his statement, but mostly from the lisp in which it came, childlike and soft, but from such an aging face.

"Why?"

"You obviously don't belong here, and you're making everyone uneasy."

"We're just dancing. Minding our own business," the lover said.

"And we paid our way. I'm a member now."

"You're not wearing a tag."

"I couldn't pin it to this outfit."

"Still, it would be better if you left. Everyone thinks so."

"You got it, buddy," from the lover. "This isn't my idea of a good evening anyhow."

"I paid and I'm staying."

Keith appeared again. "What's the matter here?" The green man bowed deeply, backed up while still bent, and spoke toward the floor. "I've asked the gentleman and lady to leave so the guests can be at ease."

"They're friends of mine. It's okay. Leave it to me."

The little man backed up a few more feet and turned before he stood upright.

"That's Pietro, the Peacekeeper," Keith said. "He tries to make everyone at ease."

"Why did he bow to you?"

"He bows to anyone he respects. That's his only direct communication other than peaceful greetings."

"Well, he sure didn't make us feel any better," she said.

"I'm sorry it's not working out for you two. I didn't know when I invited you, that you'd bring a guest. I should have been more explicit."

"I, fellow," the lover blurted, "am perfectly willing to leave right now."

"You don't have to do that. But you might skip the dance, and come down for some of the games tomorrow. Though, if you haven't enjoyed yourselves thus far, I don't imagine you will tomorrow either."

"What are the games?"

"Depends on the room you choose. The titles are suggestive. You're both intelligent, and I imagine you can guess fairly accurately. I can't just stay with you, and I hope you understand. It might cause hostility and these are my friends. They buy my books, they feature me at conferences. I have a responsibility."

"Why did you invite me? Why me and no one else?"

"You seemed different from my other colleagues. Are you sorry?"

"No. I just want to fit in." She and they knew that wasn't true, but it couldn't be *unsaid*, and she couldn't be uninvited. Now he had demolished all of her worlds.

Her lover felt the other man, Keith the Creep, had somehow violated the woman he was with, and though she wasn't truly attractive, and wasn't as intelligent as he had first believed, she was with him and therefore in his charge. "We're leaving," he said. "You can count on that."

"And on your discretion, I hope."

"We'll see," the lover said, and felt he had retrieved a little pride.

In their room, she cried deeply, so that makeup ran her face into a dissolving mask. "I must have looked *so stupid*," she said. "Damn. Goddamn. Like such a fool, showing up in a slip. I insulted them. That was it. I made light of their costumes by pretending a piece of underwear could make me one of them."

"Why do you care what they think? They're a bunch of sickos. Crazy people who can't lead normal lives, and you're crying because of them?"

"But if even they reject me, what in the hell am I?"

"You rejected them before you even entered."

"Then they're better than me. Can't you see that?"

"No. What I see is a college professor who's tearing herself to pieces over a crowd of jokers. You must want to dislike yourself. You have to really twist things to take the view you've got."

"You don't care about anybody but yourself. You never see what's going on. You even make love like you're watching your own body, or watching me watch it. You're as self-centered as any of them."

The possible accuracy of that stopped him cold. He had thought she appreciated his body. Now he wasn't certain of anything about her or him.

"Are we leaving?" he asked.

"Let's do."

She showered, dressed in a suit with padded shoulders, the one she had planned to wear to a conference session. The rest of her clothing, including the pink dress, she folded, wrapped in the garbage bag, and stuffed into her suitcase. When they checked out, her hair was still wet and her reflection was pretty ugly, as if her head were too small for her body. In her heels, she was taller than he.

"You want to carry your own suitcase," he said, though it wasn't a question.

"Glad to." She teetered toward the door and in a moment he swept up, grabbed the handle and carried the suitcase for her, angry but oddly grateful at the same time. In the back lot, the policeman recognized them as having arrived only a short time earlier, and felt he should investigate.

"You folks get driven out by the creep show?" he said, trying to be light, though he meant it.

"Yep," the lover said, stuffing the suitcases in the trunk. "We were actually asked to leave by a green runt."

"Bet I know who you mean. He's a troublemaker. We spotted him early on."

"We didn't know what kind of a conference it was," she said. "We made a mistake. They didn't do anything to us. We shouldn't have come."

"You shouldn't be driven away, though. If you don't want to go."

"Believe me," the trunk was slammed shut, "we want to go."

"That right, lady?"

"Yes."

They rode off into the fog together and they welcomed it. It seemed actually warm, and the vague, filtered lights along the highway seemed like suns that would guide them home and rise tomorrow on a new day. They held hands, and felt genuinely close, forever close. Even when they entered the backland leading to the small university town, even when the road was one-way, and absolutely dark, houses and stores closed down against the night, they felt good together.

"We're hitting it off really well, aren't we?" he said.

"Yes. Better than I thought we would."

"We had to team up tonight. That was an experience, wasn't it?"

"Yes. Scared me somehow."

"I'm glad I was with you. It wasn't pleasant, but you needed someone."

"I did. And I'm grateful."

He squeezed her hand. She held on and thought about the houses along the road, how people turned in early, snuggled against one another, maybe whispered in the dark. She sighed. "I guess life is easier if you're not alone."

"Maybe we won't ever have to be alone again."

They both thought that sounded right and good. They were suited to one another. If they hadn't attended the conference, maybe they would never have known.

In town, the nightstaff woman paced the hall. She had taken two tranquilizers and still her heart was buzzing. She could feel it, like someone had an electric charge going through her. She was going to die. She knew it just as she knew it wasn't true. This was a panic attack. Nothing more. She wouldn't die. She couldn't leave her boy alone to go the hospital, and she couldn't very well drag the child there again. Poor thing, with a neurotic mother, a crazy mother. She should've stayed at work, faced it. Then, if she went crazy, her son wouldn't see, and she couldn've gone to the hospital and then come home sedated, and he'd not know the ugly, terrified woman who wanted him raised with none of her fears. Still, she had to wake him up and get him in the car with her and drive to the hospital, because now breathing was difficult and her heart was going to stop. She wanted it to. She wanted to die rather than to feel fear like this. Unshakable, horrible, rushing fear from absolutely nothing, nothing.

The back-lot cop called his buddies for support because something was brewing out here, something big. A spikehead had kicked the green dwarf to kingdom come and now had a knife out threatening the little twerp. The cop headed that way, where the two were moving shadows in the misty light, but he didn't run, because this was a strange crew and he wanted his backup.

He heard the spikehead repeating a grunted "Bow! Bow!" but heard nothing from the shifting, smaller form till he moved nearer, and then the sound was soft, a steady mumble. "No, never, never, never."

"Bow!"

"Police," the cop yelled. "Hey! Assholes! Police."

The tall spiked man kicked out, caught the short one in the face, and then ran right over the fallen man, the sole of his shoe pressing against the throat. The cop called "Stop," but he didn't really care if the guy stopped or not, and besides, his friends were now on the scene, one taking after the running man. He himself knelt beside the green velvet punk, checked his pulse, though obviously he was alive—he was turning his head back and forth as if still saying no, while he struggled for breath. The cop called an ambulance and wondered if he were capable of cutting a breath hole in the guy's throat. He'd seen it done, and it looked easy enough. The struggling ceased and he thought there goes one little loser, but he was wrong. The paramedics arrived, said the man was alive, carted him into the vehicle and sped away to a hospital.

The cops had a talk about the group of weirdoes, about never being able to identify orangehead if he washed out the paint, and wondering if he would or not. They ambled back to their stations, feeling pretty damned good about how well they did their job. It was even sort of fun as long as no one got hurt. Pity about the little creep. He didn't give in. Had some guts, at least. The back-lot cop was glad he'd been wrong about the guy.

Inside, the nightclerk thought this was the best evening he'd ever worked. Excitement every place he looked and no trouble to speak of. These people tipped, too, or so he'd heard. And one woman obviously was drawn to him. She didn't talk at all, or maybe she did, but it was through lips that didn't move. He wondered what making love to a statue woman would be like? It gave him quickened breath. Life was damned good most of the time.

At the hospital, the nightstaff woman turned on her table, sedated now, slightly guilty about her son sleeping in the visitors' lounge. Through pleasantly blurred vision, she saw a green twisted dwarf wheeled past her, insisting that he was not harmed and should be released immediately, please, immediately. The sight didn't bother her at all. Poor ugly creature. Her life at least was better than that.

The couple went to her house, where all the lights glowed welcome to whatever moved around on such a night. She unlocked the door and he carried in the luggage. He turned out all the downstairs lights and she didn't protest, because she knew what he was doing. He undressed her slowly and lovingly, like he enjoyed unwrapping this surprise for his body, and then she undressed him. They twined together standing, while the streetlight outside softened the dark enough so that they could recognize each other. Then they lay down together, still twined, knowing that this wasn't love, but it was the best they could make together and would have to do. It might be enough.

On Sunday, the sky had settled into stillness, lowering over the city and the rolling countryside the muted gray of a common midwestern winter. In the Delmar Hotel lobby, the Fan-T-Sci group said good-byes amidst the amused or frightened gazes of incoming guests. The silver-sequined lady was the first to leave. She was wearing a tiara with three diamonds sparkling a triangle just above her wide brow. It had been presented to her at the last session, in honor of her many publications of high fantasy. But she was no fool and recognized compassion behind the gift. Now, she gathered her waning strength, and with a haughty laugh, strode boldly toward the exit, so their memory would be of grace and happiness and determination. The doorman found himself bowing as she passed, though he never stooped to such servile behavior—it wasn't one of his duties—and wondered why he felt that small courtesy not only appropriate but most pleasant.

# FROM THE HOMEPLACE

*James McMichael*

Occurrences are
runnings-toward.  From who knows what all
else time might have
sent there instead, a place is

run toward and reached and taken

up by a thing when a
thing takes place.  What it
takes for a thing to happen is a place time lets it

pose or
be posed, arrested,
placed in a resting state as clay and soured
rushes are for
one first gabled end.  Allotting things

constantly their whiles of
long or short standing, time is each stance's

circum-, its surround.
Circumstantial that the same one gabled end should
again take place as it had taken place one

instant before.  As
wide as the first, as tall,
and though time brooks few repetitions,
a second gable

too time lets take place.  Handedness

left and right affords in time a
front wall,

a back.  Before on
top of it all time lets take place as well
a wheat-straw roof,
sod over coupled rafters must be laid
grass up.

Some of a house's sides are
biased, some upstanding.  Because a

house has its sides,

so also does the air that meets them have its
clement and less clement sides.
To the sides a house is posed as are opposed as many
standing and inconstant

things as you please.
As distance is the room
away from an opposing, sided
instance or stance,
the out-of-doors

itself is sided by a house whose indoor ways makes
room outside.  Going outside,
the out-of-doors is gone out

into.
From the standstill house out
in it
(and with room between) are

hayrick and byre, a road, the moss, discrete

potato-beds, their
grass-to-grass closed hinges.
Room is by the laws of growth at

play there outside for parts related
all as one in increase in the

one thing.  Along a root
    Earthed over, earthed
           Over again,
    The rose end, heel end,
           Stolon, skin

outward through the loose mold
part by part take room.
Enlarged to *membrum*

*virilis* now in size
and now to fist, they are

parts in relation.  There are goods as

yield at the home place sometimes as at
other times
not.  Time is
equable that way.
With no parts to it in itself, indifferent,

without relation, time offers
nothing to be carried back.  Persons are
separate in time when they are living.
When certain maincrop tuberous parts go on being

missed at the hearth, back as

one again with time are persons now
outside it for good.
Against a bad
outside time,
relation

sometimes takes its sundry parts
inside.
To a first part entered in

relation with them there, inside,
the other parts are sometimes only
relatively other.
Seized as in every way

relative and to the first part's taste are such late
outside parts as are now

stew and colcannon.
As back along the tongue
palatably are carried first one

bolus and more,
        The circle of the Same surrounds
                The circle of the stripped,
        Assimilable Other,
                Pharynx-housed, tipped

down through a tenser muscle to the gullet.  Equal
each to what was wanted,

each timely part means that

apart from her
outside
are parts to be
made same, partaken, had as that one

thought is had in thinking present any
morsel she eats.  Laid
hold of when she thinks
are parts that just before were
other for her, anyone's, apportioned out

between her and her fellows.

She thinks of everything that it is
passing in its little parts.  When back at

once to those same parts are drift and
purport carried,
meaning grants the time to have
returned to her from not-yet habitable parts

just what it is she thinks of those parts as.
Until she has meant them
as that,

configurative parts are still futures,
they await being

thought about by her
as having each been fitted to its
suitable outward look.
All parts that show are in concord in their
standing over against her,

all are directed toward
what it is about them that she might mean.
As one who sees them, as one whose

self is drawn away to those
among them she sees,
no sooner is she
scattered there outside than she regains the more

that self immured in seeing them as such.

To meanings she takes part in with them, she
too belongs.
All parts that mean are

home to one still enough the same herself to be made
solute with them

inside what they mean.  Her domain

within them is the time they
take her to think.
Other for that time and
outside,
absolute,

are interrupting second parties.
High time that in his
proper person
one of them approach her now.

Others of her blood are there
around her,

inside.  His having come could pass as a family call.
She can take it as that.  So can he,
if beyond the frugal greeting she tenders
she does not speak.
To address him

puts her at risk of what might follow

straightaway.
He would be sure to answer.  It would be
colloquy then.  Irrecoverably
past thereafter would this mute

present time be.
Among such parts as
give themselves to saying, each leaves a

now-no-more-than-recent part behind.
Another now arrives,
another. Nows
track that way, they multiply,
the gaps that let each new part differ from the last

they override.
At the same time it carries

on to its own undoing, the present

keeps to itself. Resolute,
she presents the present
time and time again by keeping to hers.

Homesick for the Same, the One,
she gathers at the same time what she
watches for in him
and how it sits with her to see it. How

lavish of him that he is

there to see her. As long as she
thinks him that and goes on saying nothing,

she keeps everything at the
one same time. At the same time,
to think does not always
go without saying.
Articulations sometimes are come

out with,
they are aired,
my goodness, my
word what reach a party of the first part's

voice has for incarnate
third and second persons who can hear.
From its hollow up through the open glottal cords,

the next column of
breath she issues still gives

nothing away.  Not so,

>     The column after.  As it leaves,
>     The lappets that she draws around it
>     Make it tremble so positions of the
>     Tongue, teeth, lips and jaw can sound it

abroad. Cast
forward from her thus are parts with their
own times each.

One does not have to turn to listen.
Airborne at the middle ear,
molecular,
each damped and stronger sound prompts its allied
hair-cell to fire.  No more than a

smear at first,

the spell each sound is there for has its
onset and rise,
its temperings whose

play across the membranes no one
other repeats.
Dispersed toward him with the rest from what he
sees of her face,
the silences themselves are telling.

Of moment, every
nasal, glide and spirant,
every stop.
Time for them

all there is, these many, her express
fugitive and dative phonemes.

He has made them out.

# SMILE I. AND SMILE II.

*Jarda Cervenka*

## I.

Since I can remember I have recognized the expression of the genes she passed to me through my mother. I have the same nose as her, my grandmother, with the flaring nasal wings and wide bridge (*Pont-Neuf,* grandma laughed) and my eyes have the same contours to the upper eyelids as hers and Picasso's. My grandma's hippo hips I would have gladly erased from the genetic code and let it be lost somewhere in the abyss of the generation gap, but we both have suffered them, silently. We were united by the hips like Siamese twins; however, there remained a divide almost continental between us of the question unanswered, because it could not have been asked. "How are you doing with grandpa?" was the one.

I have the same staccato laugh as her, which I find amazing since it could not have been changed. I liked our shared interest and likings in arts and books, which used to give me much pleasure and, I believe, has been a basis of that special accord between us, an affinity which has increased in time and has become almost conspiratorial, regardless of grandpa.

Grandmother came from the old money (an expression never used in our family), which, in her case, came as a package with class and noble restraint of emotions. She has dressed with subdued elegance at all occasions; immaculately groomed she moved always unhurriedly with a calm confidence. She was a presence, which my sailing father likened to a "sleek antique cutter of teak with the brass tackle polished to gold." (He was so proud of his metaphors.)

She married penniless grandpa because of his wit, expertise in classics and good looks, too. Till his seventies these characteristics have not deserted him, including the good looks, for an old fart. I could have never, ever comprehend how grandma could have stood him for all those years; I could not fathom how she could have been so kind to him and caring to a degree almost ridiculous, at least by my book. I was not enlightened by the observation that she has ruled and micromanaged his life in everything— save amour.

At seventy, still, he would turn his head after every shapely female passing by; he would make outright primitive sophomoric remarks about the waitress and would prolong the kiss on a cheek of my schoolmate, whom I introduced, to an embarrassing five seconds. And Aunt Diane told me that he has been Don Juan all his life, "...and worse. Poor your grand-mother!" How worse I did not want to know and tried not to imagine. Aunt Diane asked me if I want to know his nickname in the school and I said I didn't.

Grandpa was a world-recognized scholar, esteemed for his translations and interpretations of scripts of Avicena and, later, for his expertise on Aesculapos and his disciples. Classical Greek and old Arabic were only part of his linguistic adventures and feats. Also, he couldn't make scrambled eggs if his life depended on it, couldn't figure out how to open the telescopic umbrella, and (evil tongues have it) he was not able to throw a baseball overhand. He had no idea about the dollar amount of his pension fund and could not figure out the difference between four-wheel-drive and all-wheel-drive. But yes, he understood the hunt for a willing female, regardless of her age, color, level of education and sexual orientation. In that sense he was multiculturally diverse and correct (as the parlance of some of today's moronic intellectuals goes), without a trace of prejudice. How could have grandma stood this man near her, I hoped to find out.

Every couple of years grandparents would journey to Austria, the birth place of grandpa and home of his cousins. The main reason was not the family reunion, really, but the visits to Viennese Opera for Strauss; it was their excursion to the realm of nostalgia. Some years I would accompany them and then we would go to see my favorite Lipizaner horses, too. Once, returning to our hotel from the horse show, I solved the mystery of grandma's marriage.

Three of us were waiting for the tram which took some time coming. Trams in Vienna were the color of that evening's flaming red sunset. The trolley coming to our station was dark blue, the windows painted over blue, big white letters on the front and also on the sides announcing this unusual vehicle to be Service-Repair-Wagon, not the streetcar desired. Since all trams must stop in every station for safety reasons, even this repair shop on wheels made its brief stop. Grandpa stepped to the door and tried to pry it open jerking the handles apart in spastic effort. Grandmother moved forward and pulled on his sleeve with quite a vigor, got him back, the tram left. I recognized grandpa's deed as surpassing his usual impracticality and as a total loss of common sense. Other waiting passengers observed the scene, bemused. At that moment I was ashamed of his stupid act.

Grandmother stood close to him, put her arm around his waist and tilted her head back to look up at him. On her face I did not see a sneer, I saw a beautiful smile radiating such bliss and happiness which would be hard to describe. I saw a proud beam of unchallenged ownership. "That was not our tram, dear," she whispered and her free hand searched for his.

## II.

Grandpa died in his late seventies, leaving his wife alone in this world for another decade. Males do that. Grandmother lived with us, then. I was in the Graduate School, but my younger brother and sister were still at home and so grandma liked her situation. She was always thinking how to spoil us and, due to her monetary situation, she could do it. Of course, we loved her. It has not been a happy time always, but one forgets things.

She was eighty-eight when the solution to her loss of many faculties was to move her to the nursing home. The only relief of our bad conscience was the physical quality of the place and excellence of the service. Her sunny private room had a balcony facing exuberant treetops inhabited by many species of birds singing at professional level. It was a Jewish nursing home, the kindest in Twin Cities.

There Grandma started to talk German, which later was replaced by French. Sometimes she switched to American to the relief of the staff. Oddly, she was aware of her language confusion.

"Why do I speak German?" she asked me.

"You went to the University in Vienna, babi." We called her babi all her life. "So it is like...well, memory of your young years."

Her loss of memory progressed in the opposite direction to the progression of time, like counterclockwise flow of a hurricane in slow motion. The last language in her life she mastered was English; before that she spoke and loved in German; her childhood was in French. So she lost English first, then German and, now, we were on the patois of Gauls. In which tongue will she greet us after her French will go? Will it be a living language? (Or Adam's verbiage he used for banter with God?) We worried.

"Why French? They tell me I speak French when I wake up. Why would that be?"

I told her about her young years in Switzerland and the boarding school in Lausanne. "Do you remember, babi?"

She said yes, but her eyes told me no. Her eyes seemed truer than her tongue, often. Sometimes her lucidity would surprise a visitor; other times she answered from some distant alien land where the sounds defied interpretation. She was in the wheelchair by then, unable even to use the walker because of her general failure to thrive and increasing frailty. So, she decided to get a job, a real job, and asked me where to start looking.

"Babi, you would have to get your legs in better shape, first," I said.

There was a lot of fantasy and illusions in our discussions. She was thinking, trying to analyze the information. Then she lightened up.

"Yes, yes, I tell you something important. Legs are a must looking for a job. Legs are!"

She was happiest when she had visitors. When we talked she held my hand and she told me I am her most favorite visitor. I hoped it came from the lucid part of her brain, since there still was such a region. Sometimes it was sad, sometimes we laughed. When I mentioned the weather outside is getting cool and Fall-like, she remarked that she would still like to feel weather, sometime.

She acknowledged the World behind her windows in lofty and exulted expressions atypical for her: "Ich liebe die Welt," she would announce, or "Die Welt ist wunderschon!" Just like that, no trace of justifiable complaints.

"Achtundachtzig," eighty-eight, I answered her German question about her age.

"Das ist genug." It is enough, she nodded, and I could not read in her eyes whether she meant *genug* to be enough, really.

I did not see any mysteries in those eyes; they were like wide open windows into her mind, no drapes on them. Sometimes, looking through these windows, I could see a scattering around of abstract objects there, objects like kindness and generosity and desire to please; sometimes from her mind-room a little child waved at me, sometimes the room was vacant, deserted.

Last Wednesday I stopped by to see babi and to bring her a few grapes. She paid no attention to the fruit. She sat on her bed still, pensive, staring at nowhere when I entered her room. Her eyes were halved as those of a brooding owl on his daytime perch, and still. Only after a while she greeted me, without the usual enthusiasm, with the usual dry peck on the cheek. She wore a sublime smile, so it seemed she has just traveled over some imaginary summer landscape of her past, or she might have planned a grand voyage, adventurous excursion into the future?

"When I become stronger in my legs, you know, I will leave here." She looked me into the eyes with only a faint determination. Was there a trace of doubt?

"You will, babi, you will." She was pleasant to look at, that day. She had on a beautiful silk and cashmere black sweater with a petit silver pattern embroidered around the neckline. Her hair was well-combed. She had a short straight cut with bangs; swankily European I thought (in comparison with the shimmering orange curls of other inhabitants of the Home), she wore elegant black pants (on her feet gigantic suede, fur-lined slippers.

Northwest Territories). She seemed lost in thought. She brightened up again.

"When I have my legs I will run home from here!" Laufen, she said which, indeed, means to run, in German. Then her face started to change and I watched the remarkable metamorphosis from the plain wrinkled chrysalis into a glorious butterfly, the smile becoming wider and brighter. I nodded, looking at her searchingly, maybe I attempted a smile. I was amazed by the miracle of anatomy, seeing her face transforming itself, radiating such a happiness and glee with the meager help of her paper-thin skin, atrophic facial musculature and eyes not brilliant any more. She was almost beautiful, again.

"And at home I will live upstairs." She pointed her mummified index finger to the ceiling and turned her head to face me fully. The glow of jubilation, of joy increased as she triumphed: "...and I will see you all down there!"

There seemed to appear a mingled eagerness and reluctance to say more, so we sat in silence.

"Then again I'll be homo. Homo sapiens, again." Her smile melted away, like the smiles of autumnal wildflowers slowly covered by falling snow.

# NECESSITIES

*Christopher Merrill*

It was either an abandoned coffeehouse or *The Pharmacy of God*—the hovel into which we had stumbled in the dark. On the shelves were nails pried from crosses in the desert, glass bottles named *The Beginning* and *The End*, bandages stolen from the wounded at Ardennes. Our spirit of adventure was a flag no one waved. What was helpless in our behavior, central to our design? The common rituals: pressing cider in a barn fire, tracking bears around the zoo, howling at the cats decapitated by coyotes. There were blues singers in the streets, stripping paint off the signs outside the beer halls. At twilight, the animal trainers sailed down the burning river in a barge, the opening chapters of aborted novels stuffed in their pockets; their wives, embarrassed in their skirts fringed with mink, were too shy to mention the smoke rising around them. These were characters without character, not mirrors of our regret. Nor are we exiles in this backwater: we are the deputies keeping watch.

•

Who are these heroes pinned to the ceiling of the den? Do they know the thieves locked in the bathroom, the pirates writing prescriptions for the spirit—which is smaller than we think? The saint bearing wood into the storeroom is only afraid of the black widows and scorpions searching for a warm place to spend the winter. Shelter is the language we are learning now, the bella lingua of the ferryman lurching out of the bar. High winds and waves, the promise of a new beginning, Americas on every page: who will write the next constitution, the next declaration of individuality? Certainly not the heroes who hiked into the mountains one morning only to discover the spring was poisoned, the oracle was silent, and the fountain pens they ordered were still on a loading dock along the burning river. And the thieves—the thieves are afflicted with a ringing in their ears: each one hears the same singer wailing at the top of her voice, warning him to sail away before the saint returns.

•

The saint's arms are chafed and strong from carrying the same bundle of wood he was given the day he entered the order twelve years ago. He leaves trails of sawdust in the monastery and the apple orchard; the daily messages he delivers to the thieves keeping watch over the storeroom resemble hieroglyphs—he never learned to read. And who can understand the handwriting of the spirits? he sometimes asks the thieves, who never laugh at his jokes. Nails, especially rusted nails, are what he collects. His favorite word is *America*, although the cider they make there is inferior, he likes to tell the thieves, to the ancient wines his friend the ferryman imports from Mongolia. Remember when the horses galloped through the orchard, through the falling snow? A posse was heading for the hills: why they wanted to gut-shoot the wild mustangs was anybody's guess. *Put the game warden to sleep!* the saint will cry the night he gives his nails to the thieves, praying they will follow him.

•

Fictions and masks and swastikas. We saw the tribesmen gathering on the ridge. Then they were gone. In the course of the fire raging across the river, in the scat singing of the women in the streets, in the false trails the bears made to trick us into following them, even in the saint's digressions—in all of this was a thread to wind into a skein, into a language and a style. Leaves fell like syllables from the tongues of rocking congregations, in tents all over America. The horses stayed behind and the walls shook. The ground was a long wave studded with flags, like buoys. No one could read the charts; the maps of our despair were useless now. And the visas or vistas counterfeited by the thieves would not have fooled anyone. Which is to say: we plan to winter here in the mountains, in a style appropriate to the age—in hair shirts and tiaras, with halberds and tracts detailing the spiritual exercises of our enemies. Our masks and fictions we will save for the summer solstice.

•

How could we have known the bridge was closed? We had the wrong tools for fixing or framing a burning river, and our stamps did not impress the ferryman. Nor did we recognize the poet waving a flag at his despair, the recruits marching in lock step over the mountain. The proclamations of the one-armed sawyers had no impact on the number of trees hauled to the mill. Who's singing now? the thieves wanted to know. Bells rang in every barn, where coyotes had replaced the cats and water troughs were freezing over. Skate home, if you think you can find ice thick enough to table discussion of the proposed rule changes until the next meeting. And don't forget to write thank-you notes to the survivors of the earthquake and the fire. Tell them they should have listened to the bears, not the saint. For there are swastikas yet to burn. And the river, the language of fire and ice, is rising faster than we imagined. If only we had called the bridgetender before we sent for you!

•

Only gestures will help us now: melting wax on the wood stove, perfuming the air in order to cut short the dinner party; smuggling sentences from *The Story of O* into tour guides of the Caribbean; teaching bachelors to pan for gold. No sense in dictating instructions to the over-populated past: they never listen. Is that musk you're wearing? Or a mask of the future? Let me count to fifty, then I'll come looking for you. Don't hide behind a tree. Hunting season has been extended indefinitely, and I have three words locked in a safe, none of which will function as a balm when the temperature drops below freezing. I also have strings of salt hanging from the rafters, a knife fashioned out of a staghorn with which to gut the albino deer framed in our sights, and enough chili powder to blister the tongue of a hasty reader. That note was for your eyes only: why did you show it to the guide? And how can you speak to the protesters in such a calm and reassuring manner? Where are you going?

# Infidelity as a Creative Act

*Mike Barrett*

You hear a medieval
cantata in stereo as
cats arch across edges

of cheap wood.  Your eyes
stray from books
square on the shelf to

the stucco ceiling and
note a body there.
How your legs shimmer!

Your mouth is full
of her—an unwritten
character—you

don't know if you're
with a lover or can't see
straight, whether

to act or cut
apart to make this
scene.  Sadly, betrayal

is a condition of both,
the description of either,
arrangement of one:

your flickering tongue, the bed,
the phone.  This exchange is
already aftermath.  You

wait for the bus, reflective,
on a street crowded
with leaves and garbage,

grey world where you set
narratives between
the objects of your love

and acknowledging them,
a way to partition
time so they never

pass you by.
Necessarily, you leave
things out: proper names,

sheets of rosehip,
an irritating lesion.  There
is an order beyond

the meagre laws you peer
over, precedents
that grind your teeth,

strain your eyes, as if
reading all night.
It demands

your presence
in a field so great
you split your vision

trying to imagine
the center.  So it goes
as someone who looks

on with interest, then
dies seasonally, maybe
an attempt to catch

you in the pain
of imitation, guilt's
shortening days, limbs

that beat time against
a seashore you've
never visited,

only heard in the prose
of a dead novelist
whose realism is how

you feel in the attic
which is desire.  You
take a ladder there,

climb down, celebrate
thanksgiving closer
to the ground where you

age, age, age.  You
are divided as you
divide, pieced together

as you labor to birth
the abstract whole.  Oh,
where in the stitch

is the song?  When standing
out from yourself you're
further inside, an echo

chamber, your voice
deep, syllables
lengthened beyond

your lips closing,
one continuous sound,
clear and harsh

as an icy coast
which gives up its
corpses only when

your letters stop
coming.  Eventually,
the tortoise quits

its shell.  You're home
and can stop chasing
the aloofness that haunts

another's body
which is the self
you can't see but

feel.  I love to
touch it, invent you
from hours,

a substitute for words
that serve as
weakness, pardon, affliction:

*mother, matter,*
*astigmatism, stigmata,*
*mate.*

# MOTHER ABOUT 26, SON ABOUT 11, RIVER IMMEMORIAL, C. 1896

*Reginald Gibbons*

Even if she wanted to go back, even if she did not have the courage to go west, she could not return home because home did not exist any longer. The *chahtah* people were finished back home, the Indian life was over. Her belly had a biting ache in it that tore at her with every step she took on the dirt roads. Sometimes holding her son's hand, sometimes walking ahead of him, knowing that behind her he had to slow his pace to hers, she walked all day.

The way before them seemed nearly empty. They retreated into the roadside weeds when once in a while a wagon or rider went by. The Negro men driving teams and wagons, the white men on horseback, the white passengers in coaches, all passed them quickly. The sky overhead was higher than the one under which they had lived back home. In all its vastness only a high circling of buzzard or hawk was alive. Itself one large open wild place, the sky not yet tamed or domesticated floated over them and over the provisional houses or commercial buildings they passed from time to time, and they felt small and at risk—the sky, the open ground, the woods, were all parts of a great predator that luckily did not seem to be paying any attention to them, for the moment.

They shared the low slow ground with beetles, toads, lizards, tortoises, snakes—creatures of the lower world. When the road was wide and sandy and bordered by open fields, then sometimes killdeer would go running ahead of them a little and take flight piping loudly, as if to raise an alarm, but not against her and her son; rather, on their behalf.

Twice they came up to and passed Negro people walking in the other direction, and she lowered her face and nodded a cautious hello without speaking, without expecting to be greeted, but her son looked at them with an open countenance. Following the paths of their own troubles, the black people looked straight ahead and said nothing.

After only three days' travel, dull walking travel, every stranger they met making her anxious, they had to stop to work in a town, in order to provision themselves anew with their payment in food for her washing clothes outside the back door of a big town house. A Negro woman em-

ployed by the whites who owned the house hired her on. Her son helped
her, and the black woman gave them both good food at noon, and filled
their baskets with food before they went on.

They walked four days and camped four nights on that food and what
else they could gather or glean and what was given to them here and
there—long days of walking on high roads and narrow dirt tracks, of
endless straight roads through endless fields, of crossing streams and ditches
and rivers. The pain in her belly was as steady as a friend who would never
forsake her. They were always arriving at what they had never seen before,
on their way to the Nations.

Then they walked through a larger town and came to a great moving
lake, at which they simply stared and before which they simply waited—
watched it move, tried to make sense of the immensity of it. Not one of the
six rivers they had already crossed was more than the tiny child of this river.
She felt the weight of her ignorance of the world. She was ashamed of
herself for not having heard of such a great water. But no one had told her.
Half hiding behind a large wooden crate as tall as she was, out of the way of
that river's-edge, white-town world, she sat near the edge of a short wooden
street that slanted down and ended squarely at the water. Her son stood at
her side.

It was a noisy place, of voices of men yelling and singing and groaning
with effort; of the chuffing steam engines of the large boats and barges
moored to the wharves, and of the strident blasting steam whistles which for
reasons she and her son could not know, would burst into full scream and
then suddenly cease. Nearby stood idle wagons, some empty and some
loaded with kegs and full burlap sacks, the mules standing listlessly in the
traces, attacked by biting flies. One wagon had four bales of cotton lying on
it, and no one even nearby to say that this property was his.

They watched the sun descending on the far side of the water toward
the low dark line of trees and land that lay below it. Twenty more great
heavy bales of cotton were standing against each other in a close bulk on the
wharf. It was late in the working day and groups of Negro men were moving
smaller lots of cargo on wheeled dollies to and from a scale where a white
man with a pencil was noting down weights in a little book. Some of the
dark men began to shift the four cotton bales from the ownerless wagon to
two-wheeled dollies, and wheel it to where the other bales stood. All the
white men and some of the black wore shoes and hats.

Across the wooden street a Negro pie woman in a raggedy dress stood
under a black umbrella, her head wrapped in a white turban, and with a

large, now nearly empty, basket of her little pies set on an empty crate before her. For such food, money was required.

A white man in clean clothes approached her and her son. Perhaps they were not to be allowed near this new crate beside them smelling of its fresh-milled wood, and he stared at them for a moment, but they kept their eyes away from him, looking down or straight across the wide waters. If she turned her head to him, he would curse her away, but, if she didn't, he might not abuse her. He lingered another moment, hovering near her, large. Her son did look up at him, and the man harrumphed and went away, and no one else approached them. They were not quite invisible, but almost. And when they had looked twice or three times at everything there was to be seen, and she had done as much thinking and waiting as she could bear to do, and even the working men went home for the day, having homes somewhere, she and her son got up and she led the way downriver, here and there across more wooden streets along the water's edge, past a variety of small boats, and finally, wearily, into scrub land south of the town, where they spent the night lying on the ground again.

In the morning, an immense riverboat was tied up alongside the dock, as if it had appeared by a conjurer's spell. Up and down a broad wooden gangplank the men who in the bright light looked dark black had formed a line and were carrying kegs and sacks on board. Her son wanted to watch, and she left him hungry in a spot that seemed protected by a great pile of barrels and crates, she told him not to move for any reason till she returned, and she went to begin asking at back doors for work. She got taken on for more washing, and walked back to the water to fetch Reuben, who obediently had not moved, but was by now aching with hunger. All that remained of the veritable city of crates where she had left him was a small pile, near which he faithfully stood, as Negro men came one and two at a time and carried them away.

Her new employer, a Negro housekeeper, was kind enough to feed them first, and gave to her son equally as to her—cold beans and cornbread and tepid tea. The woman spoke to them too loudly.

Her son stayed near when she set to work after eating. He helped her bring wood for the fire, bring water for the cauldron, stir the wash and lift the sodden masses of sheets from the cauldron. He helped her wring them, his wrists stronger than hers, and helped her hang them on looping lines held up by slanting poles, and helped her wait and rest for a while. He helped her scrub floors while the first wash dried, and helped her take the wash down and fold it for ironing inside the house. The housekeeper did not notice or acknowledge them; she only looked at the work they had done—at the washed clothes and the scrubbed floors, but the clothes and floors did not answer her. The hired woman and her son stood to one side, waiting in silence, and were at length handed more food.

She asked about crossing the river. At first, the Negro woman seemed as startled as if the washed clothes or the scrubbed floors had spoken, as if she had not thought the Indian woman capable of speech. But she softened her manner a little, and explained where to ask the Negro ferryman to take them across, and with evident pity, which made the Indian woman angry at heart, told her she would pay her in coin so that she and her son could then pay for passage—so the Indian woman had to find a place for gratitude next to her anger.

They worked on while the white family came home, ate supper, conversed and moved about in their house. Someone played a piano. The woman and her son took down the second wash from the low slack lines, brought it neatly folded to the housekeeper, and received their supper. They sat outside and ate it, speaking a few words, the sweetness of relief from hard work soothing them, but the pain always gnawing or biting hard inside the woman. They retired at dark to their sleeping place—the floor of an enclosed corner of the back porch, on a pallet of the newspapers and two old blankets the housekeeper had handed to them. It was hot that night, as it was every night. The two of them lay close and still, listening to the last sounds of white life inside the house: a few quiet voices, an occasional sound of a cupboard door or a foot on a creaking stair, then the silence of remote sleepers.

They worked a second long day and ate three meals; they slept in their corner of the porch again. In the morning they received the coins for which they had labored, and the housekeeper half-filled both of their baskets with leftover food for them and gave them a small jar of molasses. Something made the housekeeper say to them, Don't yet go. She gave them easy work that day, promising one more coin. They weeded front-yard flower beds—sitting-down work, but hot—and were given most of the hot afternoon to spend back under the big shade trees behind the house, sorting buttons, shelling peas, oiling leather harnesses, cleaning shoes, and simply resting, waiting. The next morning, with the extra coin, they set off again, and saw that, again as if by a spell, the scene at the wharves was completely changed—different cargoes, different boats. They went toward the south side of town looking for Mr. Marcellus, whom they found on a hard low dirt bank by the water, black-skinned, white-haired, thin and tall. On the bare open ground, baked and cracked by the sun, he was sitting in the meager shelter afforded by a tiny three-sided shack only large enough for his three-legged stool.

He listened and studied her face as she spoke to him with her eyes downcast, but he said he could not carry them across, he was too old now, it was too far for him. She stood before him without pressing her plea or even answering him.

After a moment of her silence, the man said, "They's reasons, too, I cain't carry you." He spat on the ground. "White folks don't wunt me carryin my trade cross river no mo." He looked watchfully out at the brown river rolling past them. "Black folks is mose cautious about it. And too it's a long way ovah and I don't have the strinth I did."

She said nothing. She did not look up at him. She took the coins, all that she had, from the pocket sewn at the waist of her dress, and held them out in her open hand.

He tilted his head back and gazed down at the top of her head, and then at the boy, whose eyes were guileless.

"Goin to fine a new home, are you," he said. With his hand so much larger than hers, his long callused precise fingers, he took all the coins but one and told her that he needed a little while to get ready. She and her son squatted side by side next to his shack in a narrow trapezoid of shade, and watched him fuss around his boat, which was to boats as his shack was to houses: a tiny low gray craft with a short peeled mast sticking up in front. The boy stood up at his mother's side and left her, to be nearer the boat, and the old man invited him close and asked him to lend a hand here and there, and began to show him the simple elements of a boat, and pointed the way he would carry them across.


Waiting, but can't wait so very long.
Waiting for some life we haven't reached yet.
A pain. Inside. Under the ribs, on the side of my strong hand.
He'll carry us across in his little boat.
I heard...of the black slaves running away north, carried across a great river. In this time, too, still bound and held, in backwoods, running from masters who owned them. Owned even the dust on their skin. Thank Mr. Marcellus.

But pain. Inside. Under the ribs of my body, in the center, up under my heart now, chewing at me, too sharp to bear when it bites.

From that place where we were sitting two days ago, the black men, white man was calling them rousters, are singing:

*Ah'm wukkin muh way back home*
*Ah'm wukkin muh way back home*
*Ah'm wukkin muh way back home, bebby*
*Ah'm wukkin muh way back home*
*Timber doan git too heaby fo me*
*no sacks too heaby tuh stack*
*all dat Ah crave fo many uh long day*
*is yo lovin when Ah git back*

Son's back—broader than mine, now. Helping Mr. Marcellus. He is one to learn.

I need a good medicine for my pain.

Oh.

Oh.

*My son. Bring me water in this cup.*

But Mr. Marcellus stops my son from going to the riverbank and dipping my cup in the river. Himself, he fills my cup, while my son holds it, from a jug in his shack, and he's looking at me.

Son is walking more like a man. He too looks; looks into me; don't; I don't want you to see inside me; where it hurts. The water is sweet.

Mr. Marcellus waving his hand to us. To stand up I feel I'm having to raise myself to the height of a tall pine; into the hot light of the sun. Son—he'll have to carry both of our baskets.

This water, how deep does it go? Under us, under the water, is the bottom world, place of snakes, place of no light, place of pain, place of *okwa naholo*. Is it deep, far down, or is it just under the boat, right underneath us waiting to *get* us?

Umh.

Deep, far down.

Umh.

Deep, far down.

Umh.

Mr. Marcellus teaching Son
He says he has to pole us
upstream
to nearby the town
before he carries us
out into the current

so that we will land
on the other side
where he wants
for us to land
Says that's how he does it
So hot now under the sun
Those big boats we saw yesterday
The men, the buildings
Place where first we stood
when we arrived at this river
so wide even a fish
couldn't swim across it
Everything's behind us now

Behind us now
Umh
Behind us now
Umh

Mr. Marcellus warns us
Says there is no town
on the other side
I don't need a town
We are going past the other side
much farther

Mr. Marcellus doesn't speak
standing at the back of the boat
pushing his pole
down into the mud
and the boat moves
only a little forward each time
this upstream way
against the river current

Now we go out over the water. No more singing, the black men singing
have stopped. Can't hear them now. Mr. Marcellus has a little sail of pale
gray cloth; a pole; or a paddle. Now the town
is away from us
We're falling away from it

It's changing and moving
Some of the houses and buildings
move in front of others
and trees walk behind them

Let me lie down now
on this short bench

*You all right? You sick? We kin go back and put in, aggin, you stay aroun and
rest up. Boy, yo mama breathin groanin like she have a heavy pain.*

*No.*
*Cross today.*
(Did I say that?)

Cross today
Umh
And in my head
a stick
is beating against a log
Son, my son, sits near Mr. Marcellus
He has two oars and a sail
Son is talking
Son is doing something for him
I can't open these eyes
Not these eyes

This river is too wide
It will be wide all day
while I'm lying on this bench in the hot sun
over the little sound the water makes
as it plays with us in its mouth
How many breaths will I have to breathe
before we arrive across this river
Mr. Marcellus is quiet-singing
That's how he's calling
on good spirits of the water
Without their help
we will never reach
the other side

*Ah nevah shall fo'git de day*
*Red Sea*
*When Jesus washed mah sins away*
*Red Sea*
*Ah nevah shall fo'git de day*
*Red Sea*
*When Jesus preached uhmong de po*
*Red Sea*

He is singing
with his pulling of the oars
The age of my father
My mother
Remember the smell
of the house at the open door
Cold bacon grease and smoke
Remember darkness
of the night
of Son's birth
Just
before he was born
snow fell at home
and it all melted while
he was coming into this middle world

Am hurt
Umh
Am hurt
Umh
How many breaths
The sun even hotter
It will burst
and rain fire on us
Tears of fire
And then it will close
like a bad eye
that can't see any more

A pain
The quiet water sound
River still has us
in its mouth
Can't close my eyes
against my eyes
Can't stop the sun
Sun is drying up my heart
In The Nations are the whole people

Up a little to look: we are lost
I thought surely we must be nearly across
But we are lost
We will never arrive
There is no shore on either side, only too much light.
*My son. Fill my cup with water—from the river, it doesn't matter*
I need more bonnet than one bonnet and we must follow the afternoon
sun, walking into the heat but toward north of the heat.
If I could sleep, but my mind
runs and runs across itself
Can't reach the other side
of itself

*Boy! See de white san?—little patch—white! We headed dar. You tell yo mam.*

There's a shore, I see it now
Water has helped us across
Son holding a small rope from the sail but the river is too wide so Mr.
Marcellus sing again please
But he is quiet

How many leaves are there
on all the stalks of corn
in all the big-house fields?
How many kernels of corn
on all the ears
of even one season?
There is time
for more thoughts than that
in this crossing

I would lie down
in some shade
for a while
not out here
Son is good
at counting
He could count
the leaves and the kernels
Sun from above
and sun from below
too
From the water
White sun
White water
Gray boat
Dark Mr. Marcellus

*Now we commin in. Boy, jump in dis shallah watuh wid dis rope and haul us in, now, good.*

The tree
is uprooted
The heart of the deer
cut from the body
Have we crossed?
Have we come so far
that no one
this whole side
of all the river
will ever know us?
Have we left
that bare hungry house
that I still can smell
where I can never
find it again?
If I could, could I?
Could I?
Oh
Must get up now
Must

Must thank
the old man
who has brought us
somewhere that
I did not want
to have to try
to find
Why was I to wander
so far
from what I knew
Why
could they make no place
for me and my son?
Something chewing at me
inside with its teeth
till it bites my heart
My heart will stop

*Thank you, Mr. Marcellus.... We fine, now.... We surely thank you, we surely do thank you, you a kind man to us.*

Gingerly the old man helped the young woman out of the bow and onto the sandy shore, where her legs were not quite strong enough to carry her through the loose sand, so he held her arm, and her son took the other. They walked her past the shade of a gnarly oak tree, where hard acorns lay on the ground, to the straw under pines, and sat her down gently with her back against a tree. The old man hobbled back to his skiff and by the bow painter he pulled it clear of the water and left it lying wet and dripping on the dry land, and gathered a small clay jug and a bundle of red cloth from where he had tucked them in the bow, and came back toward them, but stopped short, and smoothed the ground under another pine and sat there.

"Are you crying, my mother?"
    "No."
"Are you angry?"
    "I cannot tell of it."
"We are on the new side of the river."
    "Were you frightened in the man's boat?"
"I was not frightened."

"Were you worried about me?"
"I knew you would be well."
"Did you feel well in the man's boat?"
"I liked it, but I was a little frightened, because the water was at our hands, and it was very deep, and you told me that under the water is the dark world."
"Are you tired now, do you want to stop here for today, and for tonight?"
"I will stay with you wherever you wish to stay, here or all the way to The Nations."
"Do you believe we will get there, and that we will be all right?"
"Please tell me that we will get there and that we will be all right."
"I will reach my rest, and you will grow to be a fine strong man."
"What will I do?"
"You will have a farm and two mules and a pretty house, you will grow fields of corn and beans and squash, and you will hunt deer, and you will have a good wife and many children."
"What will you do?"
"I will take you to safe-keeping, where you can grow to be a fine strong man, and I will reach my rest."
"What is your rest?"
"Must I tell you?"
"I am afraid for you to tell me, but I want to know."
"I will not tell you, and then you need not be afraid."
"What should I do?"
"Come sit beside me, and give me your hand, which already is larger than my hand, and do not think about these things, but sleep through this night, you are safe here, and tomorrow we will have a good day, and we will go much farther toward our new home."
"Will we?"

This passed between them not in many words, but in only a few, and in the looks they exchanged as they sat on the new shore in the shade of the pine, and as Mr. Marcellus sat a little distance away under his tree, not looking at them.

Out on the river the boats and barges passed slowly, every once in a while. And ten great rafts of raw pine logs chained together, and six men, two white and four black, walking over them and tending them, like bugs on a sleeping hog, and a tiny cook shack built on one of the rafts, with a line of thin smoke slanting back from a tin stovepipe.

"You walkin on from here, you be all right?" Mr. Marcellus called to her.

She nodded to him, and said in a whisper that he could not hear but took the meaning of, "Thank you."

"Ah'm rest here fo while, you ought rest, too, in dis heat. You ain't goin fur, today anyhow." He settled himself against the tree and uncorked his small clay jug of sweet water and unwrapped bread and a piece of cheese from a clean red rag. From their own shade the river looked calming now, and across it, far away in the sunlight, lay white and gray spots that were the buildings they had left behind that morning. She stirred herself, pulled herself a little more upright to sit cross legged, and took out the good food from the housekeeper, bread and cold meat for her son, bread for herself. After she and her son had eaten, she beckoned him to lie down on the pine straw beside her, so that she was between him and the river, as if shielding him. She leaned her head back against the rough trunk of the tree. Her stomach quieted a little, mollified by the bread and Mr. Marcellus's healing sweet water. When she woke again, in late afternoon, the boy was asleep, his face fully a child's, without the manly pretense of the morning, and she rose up over him and looked down at him, and then looked up at the sandy landing. Mr. Marcellus and his boat were gone. There was no sound of any other person, nor any sign except the wide track in the sand where Mr. Marcellus had pushed his boat back into the water.

They began to walk westward, and somewhat north, as the roads allowed. Always the boy waited on his mother's instructions, protecting her from her own thoughts by allowing her her protectiveness toward him. She no longer took his hand; he walked behind her; he couldn't see her face except when they stopped. Over the next days, it surprised him that once in a while without warning she turned onto a smaller road, or even a narrow trail, and eventually it brought them out to a new road. She clung to her memories of her brief schooling and she would study the occasional crude wooden road sign they encountered. She spoke to no one. The boy wondered how she could know what way they should pursue.

They stopped one early afternoon, so she could rest, and did not resume their journey that day. They made a little camp for themselves off the road, under the pines. They built a fire to heat water to make a leaf tea and to boil in her tin kettle a few dumplings she made of flour and lard, and then they threw some damp green leafy wood on the fire to smoke away the biting insects. She laid out their blankets and set out a few of her things, more than they needed in order to eat and sleep, so that the night would not feel so huge against them, so that they had a little help being and remaining themselves. Remembering the history of their own unfinished journey, she said, "That was the big river, wasn't it, Son." They had seen many rivers—big ones rushing with summer storm-rain in them, and slow green ones that scarcely slid on their bellies down their muddy beds, but nothing like that big one. "We will come to our place, Son," she said softly. That it was too far to The Nations was knowledge the boy had already been given by the fierce sun and the messages of the birds in the air and the warnings of the snakes on the ground. She rested on her side, and he pretended to sleep and lay listening to her muffled groaning and saw in his mind the little boat in the middle of that river, far from any shore.

# Cache, Cabochon, Chorale

*Carolyn Moran*

Pendulous baskets of dew woven
by diamond-dropping spiders
fill with morning air as if child's breath

tested points of stress.
Nets strung to catch the dragonfly—
substantial sac of faceted coin—

veil on piquant face by silvery hands dependent—
mutant aliens occupying space—
they swing under every eave

or, still-framed like a hummingbird's
satellite dish, receive redundant signs.
If in one magic exhalation

a bubble were removèd of its planes—
only interstices and their intersections
to remain, and these demarked—

a crystal constellation:
You would have some idea
how the singer weaves a myth,

how lyre and chime commute
a silent, ringing rhyme,
how, fastened by a simple story line,

a prey's transfixed.

# THE DREAM TEAM

Massey Hall, Toronto, 1953

*Wayne Zade*


I wish they could come back
For one final concert, in the summer,
In the mountains someplace, clean,
Sober, with their mates and kids
In tow, hands not shaking
But clasping one another's,
Hugging on the bandstand,
Mugging on the bandstand,
The cool evening silver air
Like a cymbal, an ocean of bass
At flood tide, green branches
Of fingers on the keys,
The trumpeter swan in front,
And a bluebird, birds, Bird's.

# ON QUIET, SUNNY STREETS

*Wayne Zade*

That was the summer I spent
Thinking of nothing but music
Everyday.  And listened many
Blue hours, skies of piano just
Outside my window.  And far
Away, but in America, people
Were shot, in offices, on the street,
In schools, day-care centers.  You
Could watch them all many times
On TV, survivors' faces
Retelling the rage, and wonder
How, in cool rooms on quiet,
Sunny streets, tremelos
Aching everywhere in the house,
Anyone thinks of anything like courage.

# BENEATH OUR WORLD THERE'S NOTHING BUT OTHER WORLDS

*Martin Walls*

A poem is a bird that migrates from the Specific to the
    Eternal.
This time of year the weather in the eternal is warmer.

One bird didn't get there though, & crashed into the
    lawn.
Now it's cold & real, like a stone or dead leaf.
It's one of those ordinary things we think of as simple:

Slick feathers as unremarkable as damp filaments of
    bluegrass;
A broken neck, twisted in homage to branches of the red
    bud;
One upturned eye: a dim planet aligned with the bleakest
    month.

And in the hollow of its back—beneath the rib-bone
    pillars of the one true church—
Larvae are hatching from an egg-nebula, such wet &
    infinite stars.

# NOT THIS SKY

*Nancy Donegan*

In Montana a salesman told him, when you own a buffalo
plaid shirt, the less you need of anything else here.
The first fall, it could have been he who struck
the ten-point buck in his pick-up, antlers cracked
and somebody planning to eat venison for weeks.

In two years he identified eighty-one birds from his window.
The woods choked closer.  Take it easy, he told himself,
it's not going to be quick, not this time.
He would not turn to the trees massed to shore the river,
nor to Venus bright as a bomber in the western sky,
nor to the inventions he could keep in his hands: old coins
struck with winged boars, a gorgon, a boy
riding a dolphin—only to his axe and lathe.

Guns snapped in woods Sunday mornings, a harvester
droned in a field.

And not to his typewriter, car keys, the deed to his cabin,
nothing could calm him.  Not this sky melting along a ridge,
so fierce winter evenings some times he felt transparent—
barely remembering his face, a war in the desert.

In a dream he warned a deer to wait until all the lights had passed—
then it was morning and he sharpened the wood axe in his cold shed.

# ON THIS EASTERN EDGE

*Glenna Holloway*

This day, this shaper of air
to fit a skin of salt marsh scent
This sound falling through a treble staff
to merge with dark bass my soles can feel

This deep width I can't see around
or across and could wander weeks
and still be on the edge
This text, my tongue tasting of pewter font
below antique welkins

No more magnetic north, no roads
Miles turned inside out
leaving no tracks where they went

These grains, part sea salt, part drift
of forgotten continents, no line between
solid and light from this lunar ghost
never walked on, this chilled eclipse

This spiral galaxy colonized by spartina grass
This hand of mine reaching down to neap tide
to sift out my grandfathers' footprints
running before the always wind

# YIELD TO THIS

*Malinda Markham*

My daughter dreams of persimmons. What a wife she will make,
this shadow who invents no new arrangements
of dishes. She cannot serve tea. Flowers decline
in the vase her visitor offers. He has traveled some distance
simply to hear her speak. At eighteen, her beauty

unmarred as the fruit she dreamed of, so pliable I could not see her
and not think of death. After that, a girl learns to arrange
her rooms like a song. The mats without dust,
as if no foot has bruised them. I hear
she walks outside without shoes. No one will have her.

When I visited last, her doorway smelled of mikan peels dried
in a bowl. In ten years, she will comb her hair
straight down her back, nail blankets over windows
to frighten the cold. No body will warm her.
Twice, she laughed when she was young,

in a voice like marsh birds, metal against the spine.
Who will unwrap her when no one discerns
whether anything lies underneath? Unclothed,
she could be breath alone, and breath keeps nobody
warm. Will you touch her hair for me,

will you remind her I am here? She is rare
as the tree that blooms when it wills
and appears most dead in the spring. Her eyes seeds.
Will you cover her walls with silk? Beauty seen
produces more of the same. This is what it is like to be a mother

of ghosts. I fear my hand could press
right through her skin. If she sleeps, lower a cage
about her head. If she does not sleep, how will I see her?
Did you receive the fruit I sent in dry, gold grass? Oil like the sun.
Respectfully, awaiting response.

# WHO DOES NOT LOVE THE FIGURE BEFORE THEM

*Malinda Markham*

The flowers twined are copper,
tin to the touch, but you must not
touch them. The color orange
didn't change in the telling,
but the lace was all imagination,

yards added to indigo and white.
This cloth holds the wall
in place: People beneath it
speak in strung vines and irascible
twig. The last conversation
inscribed in the curve

of a leaf too sharp to ignore.
Who painted that leaf,
and why does the wind not decrease it?
Voice is much more easily
erased. Already it fades into the stem.

The background speaks, always speaking.
Where were you born? —*Blue*,
but two people talk as one: Which answer
is true? If flowers fell from the wall,
*that* would be history,

sloping toward an end. And if even then
the cloth did not change, do you see—
The rain is nothing, washes none of it
away. In time, even this touch
becomes transparent and thin. Vines
curve in the shape of their speech.

# THE SORROW AND THE GRACE OF VULTURES

*George Looney*

On trips my father said they proved grace was possible
even in this world, that memories only need
the occasional slow drag of wings to stay aloft.
Once he said they were the land itself, its desire
to dip and rise into rumors of topography
where moraines had given up thousands of years before
Indians named what was left of glacial scars and built
their own creases in land. South, there are reasons
for maps. Here, vultures drift thermals off highways,
dark angels some Italian painted. And I've seen them
hesitate over a deer with a second skin of flies,
and whispered my father's bruised name to that

bitter altar panel Tiepolo would not have placed
behind the cross. Angels, though, often carry us
to suffering. His breath when he stumbled home nights
smelled like loss. In my room, light casting his hands
on the wall, he'd open our private aviary. *Grace,*
he'd whisper, his hands settling into slow, drifting
forms, *is what keeps us from giving up.* The last trip
we took, cancer had made his hands topographical maps
of pain. He lied about remission and said faith heals
most anything. He spoke of some church in Italy
his company hid in one night. A local told him
Tiepolo had painted the frescoes that whispered

around them. Explosions brought the stained glass to
life, and in the tortured light of saints he saw them
cowering in the rafters. *It could have been the end
of the world for all they knew,* he said. The wounded
were so afraid my father and a friend opened fire.
The first bodies hung there, claws stuck in dark wood.
They'd fall later, in the silence after the shelling.
They had to shoot the rest out of the air. *It was
awful,* he said. Trapped by the amnesia of panic,

they flew without grace from stained glass to wood
looking for the rip some artillery had left in the roof
they'd come in through. Towards the end, one broke

through the flickering image of St. Francis and died.
Two escaped through the shattered monk. My father knelt
in that church and asked forgiveness without knowing
who he was asking. *It could have been God,* he said,
*or all the dead and dying.* Our last trip, he wanted
to say he'd asked the two who got out, those
desperate angels who followed Francis into a broken sky
with enough room for grace, and a landscape
that must have seemed like paradise. He said they were
still drifting adagios to hymns only the dead hear, a music
he'd have sworn was forgiveness, the way he swore
sorrow was something no angel could ever consume.

# ACCIDENTS

*David Green*

It had been fourteen years since I'd left. Fourteen years since I'd heard that voice in the night. And I still couldn't get it out of my head. The trip was my first back in all that time, the first opportunity I'd taken to go back to the place that had been my home. Ostensibly I was returning to sell the property and dispose of the remaining furniture. At least that's what I told myself. In reality I suppose I was going back to say good-bye. Not just to a place, but to a time in my life. And to Carol. To her memory, which was as much a part of that house as the bricks and mortar. And which was, more than anything else, the reason I had to leave.

The voice, or to be precise, the calls, started just after she died. Every morning for several weeks between midnight and two o'clock the phone rang. At the other end of the line was a very small, very distant voice that sounded like a desperate child. The first time she called I hung up. But as soon as I did the phone rang again. It didn't take me long to realize that it might be easier to try to sort out what she wanted than to ignore her. But I could never quite understand her. At first I thought she was saying, "It was on Acton," the street where I lived, but then it sounded more like she was saying, "It was an accident."

No one has ever accused me of being anything other than rational. Completely rational. For better or worse it's like a mantra that's followed me throughout my life. Maybe that's why I never told anybody about the calls. It would have been giving them unwarranted significance. Suggesting I may have thought they were something other than a wrong number—a confused alcoholic trying to track down her ex-husband. It's just that Carol was so different from anybody else I've ever known. She had this marvelous capacity to defy the ordinary and affect people in ways they never sus-pected. What I mean is I couldn't say it wasn't her. The voice. As strange as it sounds, I really couldn't rule it out.

The plane landed shortly after sunset. I got off and took that instinctive look around to see if any of the faces at the gate were familiar. I knew it was improbable, but the thought always enters my mind. It's just part of the routine of flying, I guess. At the baggage carousel I did the same thing. After all, I'd lived in this city for several years, so the possibility I might see someone I knew wasn't that far-fetched. But I didn't.

Outside the air was warm and still. I opened the door of the first taxi in the rank and tossed my bag on the seat. For a moment I wasn't sure if the driver was even taking passengers, but then he turned down the radio and leaned back, tilting his head in my direction.

"Take the loop in on the east side to the Jackson exit," I said. "I'll tell you where to go from there."

He called in his location and then crowded into the flow of traffic paying little attention to the cars and crosswalks in his path, slowing only when he came to a stoplight on the airport road. As he waited for an opportunity to turn he glanced at me in the rearview mirror. "The northeast," he said. "I'll bet you're from the northeast."

"You're right," I said.

"I went up there once back in the eighties." He leaned over the steering wheel and looked left.

"Really?" I asked, "What did you think of it?"

"It was all right, if you like cold weather." He turned the steering wheel slowly, anticipating the traffic, and then inched out to the right before accelerating around the corner.

"It does get cold."

We crossed through another intersection and proceeded up an access ramp to the interstate. "You know the thing I missed most when I was up there?"

"What was that?"

"My apartment. It's funny, isn't it? I felt like I had abandoned an old friend. I kept thinking back to the hours I'd spent sitting by the window looking out through the trees at the garden. Or going over every detail of the fixtures in my mind. The knob on the door to the back porch. The wind chime. The crack in the ceiling."

"We grow as accustomed to things as to people," I said.

"To what?"

"To things as to people."

"That's right. Maybe more."

He reached into the glove compartment, took out a pad of paper, jotted something down, and then slipped it back in and shut the door.

"I was on top of things when I went there," he continued. "Everything was paid for. Everything was working. First thing they do is hit you for a hundred dollars a night for a room while you're looking for an apartment. Then when you find a place it's rent, deposit, and a fee all at once. Then the engine on my car started smoking, and I thought, 'Hell, out of state plates. They're going to take me for a ride.' And they did. Then my new hundred-

and-fifty-dollar shoes started squeaking. It may not sound like much, but think about it. You go in for an interview wearing your suit and squeak your way up to the person to shake hands. Not that I ever had an interview. Four years of night school. A master's in business administration. And not one call. Can you imagine that? Not one damn call. Excuse my French."

He looked in the mirror. I shook my head.

"The worst of it is that everybody is always telling me how lucky I am because I know a lot about the ins and outs of business, that finding a job should be easy. That's the worst thing somebody can say. Because it's not easy. I'm living proof of that. After a while you don't know what to do. Throw good money after bad, or admit you were wrong and cut your losses. But then where do you go? You can't take a minimum wage job because your rent for a one-bedroom apartment is seven-hundred a month and minimum wage is only nine-hundred before the government gets a hold of it. The car alone cost me five-hundred to fix. What about food? Insurance? Gas? The whole time I was there I felt like I was drowning. I'd given up everything to go there and was living on what savings I had. Every Sunday I'd buy the paper and circle the jobs that were right for me. Then I'd type up a letter and a copy of my resume for each one. On Monday morning I'd get in the car and go by the places in person. Most of the time I never got past the secretary. When I'd ask to speak with somebody higher up, they'd tell me they were in a conference, or make up some other story. Two or three times they misspelled my name in the rejection letter. I'm talking about major corporations and even universities. You feel guilty like you're being too forward, but if you don't make an effort, nobody knows who you are. You're a leper. You're a modern day leper. People are out there going about their lives and you're sitting in a room writing letters no one is ever going to read. Workmen next door are whistling as they put up scaffolding. Nurses are driving by on their way to work. Kids are going to school. And what are you doing? You're sitting in a room writing letters to people who can't even spell your name.

"In the meantime, like I say, the compressor goes out on your car. You sit on your sunglasses. A filling comes loose from your tooth. Things go on breaking. They don't stop breaking because you don't have a job. They don't declare a moratorium because you don't have enough money to get them fixed. Jobs you thought you'd never consider you suddenly find you can't get. Then on the radio they're talking about how good the economy is. The stock market is booming. All the people that have money are making a lot more.

"What I said about no interviews wasn't exactly true. I did have one, but it didn't count. I was like one of the extras in a police line-up. They already had their person, but they were obliged for some convoluted reason to go through the motions. That's why I say it wasn't really an interview. They called me in and got my hopes up so they could feel good about themselves, so they could go to bed at night knowing they had been fair. While I was living in an empty room eating soup and potatoes. Wondering if I was losing it. I'm serious. One night I was sitting on my cot with nothing to do and I noticed my ties hanging in the closet. I blew as hard as I could to see if I could make them move. I couldn't tell if they did or not, so I blew again, and then again, for about ten minutes, and then I realized just how bad things were. I was sitting in a room without a job blowing on my damn ties. You know what I'm saying? You start thinking 'Hey, what's crazy anyway?' You know? Where do you draw the line?"

I suddenly realized he had asked me a question. "It's hard to say," I said. "Maybe it's all just a matter of perspective."

"Perspective. Yeah."

"They committed Christopher Smart because he prayed in the street."

"Even though God is supposed to be everywhere."

"Exactly."

"At the time I was living in this nondescript apartment house in an urban suburb called Middletown. And I didn't know a soul. Not a solitary soul. I could have keeled over and nobody would have known the difference. Anyway, one afternoon I was outside fiddling with my car when this old guy from the ground floor came out. Dominic they called him. Used to work in a garage down the street. He'd been retired for fifteen years but he still liked to tinker with cars. So he checked a couple of things out for me and we started talking. He'd been a refugee and had lost his wife to cancer in the fifties. I commiserated and told him my story. About the problems I'd had finding a job. We both agreed that the world was in a pretty sorry state. Then he kind of lit up and asked me if I wanted to try some wine he had. It was already late afternoon and I figured what's the harm, you know? His apartment was like a trip back in time. Vintage Old World with this strange smell of acetone or something. There was a tall bookcase covered by a white cloth hanging from thumbtacks. In the little kitchen was a pine sideboard with a lot of colorful plates and a table covered by a red and white checkered cloth like you might see in a European restaurant. The curtains were all closed and in the semidarkness I noticed something I hadn't noticed in the light, that he had these bright red hands. Bright red, like he was always washing them.

"I sat down at the table. He poured me a glass of wine, something from the old country, and then stood next to me with his hands on the back of a chair, smiling, waiting for my response. But just as I was taking a sip of the stuff we heard a car screech to a stop and then howling in front of the building. When we got out there we found a small stray dog frantically dragging itself in circles just inches from the traffic that continued to speed past. Its back had been broken and it was bleeding at the mouth. Old Dominic, he was pretty upset. He picked the dog up and held it in his arms. Blood was frothing from its nose and the sleeve of his shirt was soon red almost from the shoulder to the wrist. The dog continued to kind of cry and shake convulsively but seemed to put its trust in the old man. It must have known it was dying and perhaps that that was the price it had to pay for a moment of kindness in this world. We got in my car and drove a couple of blocks to a vet's who gave it a shot that put it to sleep straight-away. Dominic insisted on paying for the procedure and kept fretting about the blood stains on the seat of my car, promising to clean everything in the morning when the light was better. That night the poor guy couldn't sleep. I could hear Bartók coming from his apartment until I drifted off about one. When I woke up in the middle of the night it was still playing.

"The next morning about the time the traffic is heaviest I heard an engine roar and sputter behind the building. It was Dominic. He was going out the driveway on a backhoe that had been left at a work site in the alley. By the time I got out front he had planted the thing broadside to the traffic and was digging a trench across the street. The long arm of the backhoe jabbed and scratched spasmodically at the pavement, like the tail of a mechanical scorpion, and then came up cradling big chunks of asphalt and then a layer of bricks and then orange clay and rock. People were on their horns and shouting, of course, but he just kept digging away. After about fifteen minutes he'd made a hole all the way across the street three or four feet wide and three or four feet deep. He knew what he was doing, I'll say that for him. The police eventually showed up and hustled him off in a car with the lights going and everything. John Dillinger. Al Capone. I remember he had his arms up in the air like he'd just won a race or something and was smiling the same smile he'd had when he was waiting for me to taste his wine. He didn't care what they did to him. Old guy without a wife or family. They could have tortured him and he wouldn't have cared. Because he had made his point. He had stopped them. He had stopped them all. Every one of those S.O.B.'s. After all the commotion had died down and they'd put up detour signs, it was perfectly quiet out there. For a few hours anyway. Then the city crew showed up to fill in the hole and put a layer of asphalt over it. Soon the traffic was as bad as ever. And old Dominic was still in jail. He never got a chance to hear the quiet. But I think he was happy. I mean the feeling of tearing up that road must have been worth it. Knowing that he had that power. There was a lot going on with him. I found all that out later. And tearing up that road meant far more to him than I could have imagined when I saw him out there. It was a choice he'd made, a conscious choice, to determine what would happen to him. To have that power. That's all he wanted. For him that was happiness.

"As it turned out, this old man hidden away in a basement apartment in a working-class suburb who had fixed carburetors for twenty-odd years in a neighborhood garage had been a guard in a concentration camp. His name wasn't Dominic at all, but Miroslav. During the extradition proceedings the papers said that as many as a hundred thousand people had died there. A hundred thousand."

"Makes you wonder," I said.

"It does. It really does."

"That's the strangest story I've ever heard."

"The strangest? I don't know about that," he said and then paused for a moment. "No, I think the strangest would be something that happened to me down here. Just after my divorce. Oh yeah, I was married once. Hard to believe? It's hard for me to believe. Given that I'm not the easiest person to get along with. I know that. But that wasn't really the problem. No, I can sum up the problem in one sentence. She was the kind of person who'd spend sixty dollars on an aerobics class and then park in the handicap zone at the store so she wouldn't have to walk so far. I just couldn't live with somebody like that. Call me particular. Maybe I'm too particular. Maybe other people don't have a problem with that sort of thing. I don't know. I'm not other people. But I don't see how anybody can live like that. Makes you wonder why people get married in the first place."

"The triumph of hope over experience," I said, assuming he was familiar with the phrase.

"I'll tell you one thing though, one thing for certain," he said. "If I'm going to be alone, I'd a whole lot rather be alone and be by myself than be alone and be with somebody else. You know what I'm saying?"

He leaned over and shifted a lever on the dashboard. "Cool enough for you back there?"

"I'm fine," I said.

"She wasn't exactly a sweetheart of the rodeo, but she wasn't that bad either. I mean looks-wise. I know you can't have everything. I know that. I do think about that. But you can have happiness and I wasn't happy. Not that I could ever tell you just exactly what that is or how you know when you've actually found it. Maybe it's when you're thinking of winter and you imagine a deep blue sky instead of gray city streets. Maybe that's happiness. I don't know. Whatever it is I can't say I feel that way all that often. Not anymore. But I make up for it by looking for the happiness in others. And when I find it I feel a little something of what they feel. That's all I care about. That's enough for me. Sharing someone else's happiness. Even with a stranger. Especially with a stranger. There was one in particular I'll never forget. Like I say, it was the summer after my divorce. I was working construction at the time. Well, to be accurate, 'heritage reconstruction.' Or at least that's what they call it. We had this job downtown. A lot of them downtown, in fact. This one was a series of town houses owned by the same management company. So we were down there for four or five months. I always liked it down there. The old trees and the brick sidewalks. You know the city?"

"I used to live here."

"The houses were on Bristol, and because my wife had gotten the car in the settlement I had to take the bus, the fourteen I think it was, and walk a couple of blocks down to the site. Once or twice a week right when I was getting off, right about four, I used to see this woman going into one of those brick row houses on Acton. Between Fifth and Sixth. The first time I saw her she had just gone down the steps and was looking over her shoulder watching the street apprehensively, fearfully, you know, as she waited for the door to open. I looked right at her and she looked right at me. The Doris Day type with sky blue eyes and bright red lipstick. She had blonde hair, but was wearing a scarf. I can still see her standing there just below the level of the garden. Her eyes among the roses. Her blue eyes. I knew what she was doing. I could tell by the expression on her face. And she knew I knew. She was looking for happiness.

"Anyway this went on for weeks. It even got to the point where I'd say hello to her when I passed her somewhere down the block. I only saw her with the man once or twice. They seemed happy enough. Maybe she had found what she was looking for. He seemed like a decent sort of guy. But I don't remember him as well. It's the woman I'll never forget. Those blue eyes.

"Then one week I didn't see her. In fact I never saw her after that. But I did have this dream. I dreamt she was driving on a road in the mountains and stopped to ask me for directions. I told her to turn around and go back. I don't know why, but that's what I said. And I put so much stock in that dream that I would have told her about it if I'd had the chance. I would have stopped her on the street and told her. That's how strong the feeling was. And then two days later I saw her picture in the paper. She was killed when her car went off the road on East Mountain. Can you believe that? You probably think I've made this up or imagined it or something. But it's the honest-to-God truth. Right off the road without a single skid mark. No attempt to stop. I know because I went up there. I took a day off from work and went up there. I walked up and down that road for over an hour studying the scene from all different angles, trying to find some kind of clue, some kind of reason. But I never did. I never did find out what happened. That was fourteen years ago this summer, but I remember it like it was yesterday. Makes you wonder, doesn't it? I mean about happiness."

I didn't answer. The light from the headlamps of approaching cars flashed through the dark interior of the taxi like startled ghosts. After a few minutes the road curved to the south and we entered the hills just outside town, climbing a long, steep grade as the red taillights of the cars ahead of us vanished over the top of the ridge. A crescent moon was now clearly visible in the pale green sky. For the first time since leaving the airport I noticed the radio. The sunny voice of a disc jockey, so out of place in the darkness, continued speaking as another song began. Over the shoulder of the driver I could see his fingers tapping the beat of the music on the steering wheel.

"You should write those stories down," I said.

"I plan to," he said. "I plan to do something with them."

# HARMONICAS

*Laura-Gray Street*

On a branch two buzzards
mirror each other,
their wings outstretched,
drying dew in the wind

perhaps. Or they're courting.
For hours, arguing
the silent strain, like heavy
black wool on the shoulders.

I should go somewhere
and look for meaning
that way. Weight,
the way of testing the true,

the durable world . . .
A man with harmonicas
once joined my table
on break between sets—

show tunes, a round of gospel
to prove he was saved.
Or so he told me, placing
a one-hundred dollar

wood body in my left hand,
an eight-hundred dollar
steel body in my right.
"Weigh the music," he said,

"the relative values of sound."
That easily we should know
bad from good, good
from great. Not the years

of instruments the man
explained he threw away
before learning
to file his reeds and test

music with a meter,
matching, face to face,
note to true note. Then
he told me a joke–*the*

*jim said to the spic–*
that proved he was human.
"That's bad," I said,
needing a moral; adding,

"I met God once,
while I was running.
Near home, I heard him
snarling: *Runner!*

*Run faster little girl–*
*Runner!* I recognized
his long knotted hair
and beard; his defecations

in the yard; his bulk hitched
against a rusty camper,"
I said, measuring steel
against wood, "The neighbor-

hood schizo, drunk; off his
meds. I ran faster, his wind
at my back." "Back when,
I'd played and they all

came to hear me. Paid
good money too,"
the man with harmonicas
said, meaning more

than the bar's bad lighting
could disguise, or his
back-to-business riff
when he saw I couldn't

care less . . .
If we should meet
again—you and I, I
and you—spare me

this, against your better
judgement: light good enough
for shadows; wind to run on;
and the counterpoise to rest

my arms on the ledge
and watch the buzzards
finally folding, two

overcoats shrugged onto pegs.

# POTTERS' FIELD

*Laura-Gray Street*

*—a piece of ground reserved as a burial place for strangers
and the friendless poor*


                    Then the storm
furls like a snapped sheet, folds neat
into the eastern drawer,

and it's an evening for sunset collectors,
we like to say.

Sky deepens
                from flush to muscadine
like the cherries, tree-ripened.

                        *Except where crows peck: pits dangle,*
                        *withered stars on black stems.*


Let us rehearse a lifetime's
opalescence:
                what we remember
folds straight-seamed with what we will;

                what we will,
that white cotton, wears smooth with cleaning.

                        *We remember the blood that ran*
                        *through the birds of our fingers.*


So we tease thread
through cloth until it gives

into another stitch.  Rise and fall,

pucker and smooth.


Thread knotted
like a branch of forsythia; thread knotted
like the lilac or buddelia.

Our necessary scraps and buttons.

*Only field stone and rotting log
mark our shed snake-skins, dull scales,
dark holes our mouths moved through.*

But useless,
uprooting old losses. Let them lie,
numerous, anonymous,
as if they crept off this life when their shadows
shrank to toadstools at noon.

*Even here, engrossed in the remains
of sun, barefoot, abstracted, disarrayed,
you won't see—
We are the anthill's
erratic swarming at your instep. We are
the opportunistic weeds you pick:
bindweed, loosestrife, alyssum.
We are the ground wasps
burrowing chambers in your shade.*

# What Cannot Be Fixed

*Jill Peláez Baumgaertner*

Anything can be repaired,
the violin-maker says,
except for woodworm
or the violin inside the
fire-melted case.

A violin is more than its own strings'
sound, the wood thin and flexible,
loose for sympathetic resonance,
leaning into the cello's timbre,
leaning into your own voice.

Things can go wrong, he says.
The glue must not petrify
the instrument. Even the soundpost
sometimes eats the wood and begins
to push its way through.

Or the fingerboard can loosen
and warp the soundboard.
Or a person changing bad strings
can release tension
so fast the soundpost shifts.

Or the instrument can be fraudulent,
aged with artificial nicks,
fake repairs. But most can be fixed
again, he says, the last button
missing on his shirt.

Repairing a violin is like stitching
something which is torn,
he says, rocking on his heels,
unwrapping necks, wood,
damaged violins to pass among us.

We handle them warily, uncertain
how to touch these specimens
of imperfection, blackened by fire,
crushed by the car's fender,
caught in the flooded basement,
frozen in the abandoned car.

# THE STRING SECTION SKINNYDIPS

*Jill Peláez Baumgaertner*

After midnight the lopsided Irish moon is heavy
with light and the rocky path to the lake is as clear
as water. The brass players are still drinking
up at the Big House of the Artists' Centre.

The mist fills in the gaps between the hills,
hovers over the far side of the lake and the cellists,
violists, the violinists and bass players strip
to their knickers and beyond and enter the chill waters.

Three writers stand on the shore as still as tree
stumps and watch. Cut off by the edges of a canvas,
the lit greyness would be incomplete,
an environment one could choose to enter or exit,

and that is not the way it is at all.
There are no choices in this complex of factors.
We all have our places and play our parts.
I stand watching the mysteries that

even Yeats could not pin down. The only way
to hold it is in memory, the splatter lap of water
distinct at midnight, the cold air filled with moonlight,
the rocks through my shoes' soles, the slightly drunk poet

standing next to me, the sober conductor
near the water's edge, trying to see the naked girls
through his thick glasses, the mist, the dimness
making him stand very still, concentrating—

like that one second tomorrow before his baton bursts
the music into bloom. Listen. The music has not
yet started to unfold. The violinists are floating,
breasts barely visible. The music is a wrapped satin bud,

waiting, waiting.

# Natalia Ginzburg's Dream of Music

*Peg Boyers*

> Never ask my name.
> —Lohengrin

I sleep at the opera.
The problem is the music.
I just don't get it.
I am a person who should *love* music.
I'm sensitive enough—and smart.
You could say I'm an artist.
I was *meant* to love music.
Perhaps it's *music* that doesn't love *me*.

Did I inadvertently rebuff it
the one time it paid me a visit?
Maybe, through some tragic mistake,
music was on its way to me and got sidetracked,
distracted into landing on some other spirit.
Perhaps by some lapse
I missed its presence
and it slipped away unnoticed.

Once, on a tour of the Forum,
I ducked into a temple to say a prayer to Orpheus.
I asked him to descend on me with his lyre,
thrill me with his song.
I was a siren on the ruins, waiting to be ravished.
But my prayer went unanswered.
Later, I learned it was mis-addressed.
My fate, musically speaking, was sealed.

*Jealous Apollo, god of music,*
*accept my corrected prayer!*

It's not that I don't try.
I do.
Year after year, I renew
for the season
because I love *being* at the opera.
By now the opera house itself is dear to me,
our box the host of countless
stolen naps and covert dreams,
red velvet seats perfect for opulent reverie.

Sometimes I approach the opera with genuine determination.
I concentrate hard on the voices,
the interplay of plot and histrionics.
For a fleeting moment, I imagine
my struggle is paying off, that music's
seduction is but a note away.
I *almost* hear what others hear.
I know that I am about to achieve tremendous pleasure.
This pleasure will be as immense and fathomless as the sea.

Next thing I know,
I'm drowning in sleep.

In my dream I am Elsa with her Wagnerian knight,
his breastplate resplendent with theatrical reflections,
helmet protruding virile horns.
He sings me the conditions of our union.
I trill my ecstatic compliance.
I am at home in mystery.
I don't care who he is or what to call him.

# THE SIX WAYS

*Terence Winch*

First there is entering by going backwards,
reversing the drift into museums and airports,
where we tend to forget or disintegrate.
All movement begins to rewind.
As we stare at the past, the future's
yellow light x-rays our memories.

Second is the use of satellite languages
that give the impression of a life lived
in sumptuous splendor, as in recordings of
ancient philosophers actually speaking.
Radio signals help, as do hieroglyphs
and expensive costumes. Everything must
either be translated or transparent.
There is a map ceremony in which smuggled
inscriptions reveal our sexual fantasies.

Not understanding is number three.
You crash, you lose your gear,
you become a master of confusion
and begin to understand the differences
between a temple and a shrine.
You are berated by unknowing
voices saying "The more I ate
the more my appetite grew."

Reconstructing where you have been
is the fourth way. You will need
a wig, a human skull, and gold earrings.
You must uncover the chamber where
your parents first noticed the circular
incisions on their arms. You must rob
tombs, smash pottery, sing to your concubines.
The entrance is sealed, but you will find
a bone and a mirror to unlock the door.

Number five is pretending you are a dog.
You make yourself feel such anxiety
that it actually seems as though your ears
are moving back and forth. You sit for
long periods. You also stay.

Close examination of the clothing worn
when you were a child is the sixth way.
There should be a jacket made of felt
and a ridiculous hat made of tinfoil.
You should use gold spoons to bury
your pants under the tree of life.
Every morning when you wake up
you should feel your status rising
like the mist over the mountain.

# THE MEN ON THE WALL

*Maria Terrone*

Brawny men on the wall hoisted iron, their steel
muscles rippling. Painted before the second war
by WPA artists, the mural celebrated work
and freedom, cities rising bolt to beam, the red-
blooded and able-bodied. At 17, I felt strong, armed
for my summer job at the VA, ready to hear

and transcribe the words of vets—not conquering heroes,
but mental prisoners of war. Tapes awaited in a steel
box, but I was brooding over the one-armed
elevator operator on the way up who wore
medals against his heart, and the headline I read
in the lobby: *Mekong Bombed Again—The Work*

*of General Westmoreland.* They say a woman's work
is never done, and mine was to hear
the cries of drowning men who thrashed in the red
well of my ear. Each day I was linked by cords of steel
to a Dictaphone, a Pandora's box of secrets—war's
aftermath, terrors that rage long after the arms

rust. Each day, the pain: head, neck, arms
and fingers exploding until I went numb from work;
the tapes in my out-box rising, casualties of war
stacked like two-by-fours. Did the other typists hear
the same kind of stories? Did they have to steel
themselves as I did? Did the women also blush red

in pity and shame for men who fought the Reds
and survived, only to jab needles in their arms
to join the dead? I glanced around, saw steely
eyes fixed straight ahead, feet like pistons working
a machine. Some veterans complained of hearing
voices; they said the doctors' drugs helped but wore

them out...No one in my unit ever talked about the war.
Our ballroom-dancing boss flounced up the rows, her red
dress a swirling flag.  Even now I can hear
those tapping heels, see her gather tapes in her arms,
then waltz out of sight.  When I remember that work,
I picture the hungry, stalking wolf who steals

the red-hooded girl.  That fall, eaten alive by war, I begged
God to hear me and work two miracles: melt steel
arms and save the men who now speak from a black wall.

# WATER RITES

*Marilyn Krysl*

In a circle of elms near the stone farmhouse, my grandfather had cemented a shallow pool. I entered this cylinder of shade, lay on my belly. Fish slid in lazy loops. Domed light arched over this sphere. Only the fish moved, in that other world, the one under water.

I was four. I had heard my grandparents talking about how badly we needed rain. Their faces registered their concern. I would have to do something to help them. But what? I picked up a twig, dropped it in. The twig floated at the center of concentric ripples. Then, on the opposite rim, something thick and dark slid down to the water and in.

Over it the water closed.

I had seen four legs, a tail.

A breeze stirred the elm leaves. I sat up. Beyond the rim of shade where there had been sun, the grass darkened. Now a god shook the thunder rattle. I had the distinct sense that my toss of that twig had set something large and above us in motion. I leapt up and ran toward the house. My grandmother was kneading dough. Her presence amidst the scent of yeast was reassuring. Bright bursts of speech flared from me, and she nodded. The creature, she told me, was a water dog. They were shy, she said. I felt a swell of friendliness: so was I. They resembled lizards, but lizards preferred heat and drought. Water dogs were heralds of storm. They wove themselves in and out amidst the slippery fish. Then, with a magic flick of their bodies, they wafted this watery atmosphere up to heaven so that it might come down to us as rain. As she spoke, we heard the tick of the first drops.

Centuries before this, my ancestors crowded around the priest at Mt. Lykaios. He prayed, and they watched the slender branch of an oak tree in his hand. When his prayer ended, he offered the branch to the pool. It floated, then began to sink. Something resembling mist rose above the water. Those of my ancestors who were there said the air turned electric. A jagged streak of light cracked across the sky. Afterward an intensity persisted where the streak had been, as though that heat had left its imprint. Then all present felt the shudder of thunder. A few minutes later the downpour began.

Summoning water is an ancient rite. The priest and I had invoked the
serpent goddess.  In the Vedas she is Kadru, to the Babylonians Kadi,
goddess whose body is snake, with breasts, and the shoulders and  head of a
woman. Watery form of the energy Hindus call *sakti*. She of the waters
above and below the world, waters whose energy moves in a serpentine
pattern. Myth tells us she separated a length of this energy from her,
fashioned it into a wavy slither like the pattern in water. She made a slickness, but with substance. And with this slipperiness pleasured herself.

Her offspring are nagis, serpent genies sliding away from her, sinuous as
the water itself. The Greeks thought the nagis ugly: coarse bodied, reptilian,
scaled—like the water dog. But the nagis' ugliness confers magical properties. Like water letting go a ripple, the nagi's skin slides off, floats away,
dissolves. The nagi, bringer of rain, embodies our longing to be reborn.

I have come to Tobacco Caye to pay my respects to Ancestor Water.
Lying  beside  the coral reef off  the coast of Belize, this Caye is so small you
can walk across it in five minutes. The shore is strewn with feathers from
cruising Frigate birds, palm branches last night's storm blew down. Where
the shore slopes down,  a ridge of rain beaten sand. Stones beside the pier
gleam. The water itself seems scrubbed clean.

I walk into the immensity of water. Entering the sea feels like entering
another body. "Women's sexual organs," the Diola sing, "are full of water."[1]
In Sumerian *a* meant both water and sperm. Some *sakti* from that first sea is
still in me, and in you, regardless of our gender. I dive down. *Holocentrus
ascensionis'* ribbony fins resemble pastel chiffon. Groupers are slices of
sunlight, submerged. Below the coral, grass beds nurse fish, and where fish
graze and defecate, the coral grows faster. I weave amidst the feasting, and
feel at home. I too have come to feed and be fed by this feeding world.

Afterward, I lie in the shade. *Body of water*, we say. "Let us not impose
doctrines upon the landscape," Natalia Rachel Singer writes, or "metaphors
of the body."[2] I too would not attribute to nature merely human capacities.
But if we cannot use the word *body*, how then speak of our long love affair
with water? "Nowadays we prefer to speak of the environment," writes
Deborah Tall, "but it too, in its original meaning, is what surrounds us,
rather than what we are inextricably involved in."[3] So call it inextricable
involvement then. In *The Spell of the Sensuous*, David Abram describes this
involvement as a kind of "reciprocal encounter."[4] Living systems continuously perceive and interact with surrounding systems, making finely tuned
adjustments. With every sense perception the jig changes, partners grooving
with each other even as they reshape the groove. We and the world hail each

other—thanks for the news!—and like the shrug of a jacketed shoulder, shift our chemical balance and proceed.

Just as I feel water against my skin, water registers the space I take up. I float, and water holds my weight. I drink, and water tastes me. Merleau Ponte called this web of reciprocal encounter the world's *flesh*. Streams, springs, waterfalls and seas of this flesh pulse forth their fluid energy. "They *are*," Mercea Eliade writes, "and they are *alive*."[5] Why not say *body of water*?

And why not call ocean our ancestor? Fluid and androgenous, this bubbling forebear gave birth, fashioning the appropriate elders. "When they went ashore," Rachel Carson writes, "the animals that took up a land life carried with them a part of the sea in their bodies."[6] The signature of that original parent is still in us. Human body hair is not arranged in the pattern of other apes but in the pattern in which water's mantle flows over our bodies as we move through it. Our bodies are three quarters water, the proportion of water to land on the planet. And sodium, potassium and calcium combine in our blood in almost the same proportion as in the oceans. We're mostly water, with a pinch of salt in our cellular pockets, sloshing from one liquid decision to another.

I was three when my mother took me to the Pacific. The water, rocking, refracting light, reminded me of certain green glass bottles. This was color ceaselessly moving—and sounding. Ocean's voice was guttural, Orphic. When I closed my eyes, its moaning rippled through me. Sound waves replicate the ocean's wave form. The rhythms of our speech echo the liturgy of pouring water. We say of a brook that it babbles, and why not: language, after all, is another bodily gesture rising out of what we are inextricably involved in.

I stood before this ancient, uttering elder. Egyptians imaged masculine and feminine combined in the Nile's floodwaters as the anthropomorphic goddess Hapi. The Babylonians projected Apsu and Tiamat, waters whose currents mingled in a single mass. Homer described Oceanus, a powerful river in amorphous space where there was neither sky nor earth. Tethys was figured as the female, but her spiraling mass could not be distinguished from the course of Oceanus itself.

Before me in one body, resounding: Grandfather Ocean, Grandmother Water. I understood this forebear was alive, and very old. Ocean endures, and, at the same time, the huge fact of these waters seems to cancel duration. Sea's ceaseless moving seems to neutralize time. Confronted with such persistent immensity, we can imagine nothing before it. "Water," Elide wrote, "precedes all forms and upholds all creation."[7] *Neither Non-Being nor*

*Being existed then,* intones the *Rgveda. Neither air nor the firmament above existed. What then was moving with such force? Was it the deep and fathomless water?*

Soulful, ruminating, the great body spoke to me. It listened, knew me. I felt naked, watched and heard in every cell. Later I would learn Sardinians worshiped certain springs and held ordeals there by which a person's truthfulness was tested. That the Vedas assert that water seeks the truth, that waves of the ocean keep away lies. But I knew instinctively that day, that I dared not dissemble in her presence. I was everywhere seen, heard, known.

And if water heard me, then I might speak with it. I stood on the beach and answered this ancestor with the same *ur* syllables I heard rising out of her. I hissed and groaned. I was murmur and lament and roaring power. When we returned to the Midwest, I continued this conversation with water. One day I stood on the couch in my grandmother's parlor, looking down behind it,  listening to my mother and grandmother talk. When there came a lull in the conversation, I announced that there was a stream running behind the couch.

"Don't tell lies," my mother said.

"It's underground," I said. "You can't see it."

"And what does it say?" my grandmother asked.

"It's saying you should believe me!" I replied.

A generation later,  this sense of water's knowing came to my four year old daughter. One afternoon she squatted at the lake's edge, listening intently. Suddenly she swung around. "If you tell a lie," she said, "the water will hear you."

Here on the Caye, I think of John Muir laying down on the Sierra Nevadas' granite in order to "think like a glacier." But to think is not the same as to know. Scientists investigating water's knowing have found it sensitive to even very slight changes in electrical and magnetic fields. In the thirties Giorgio Piccardi found that the rate of chemical reactions taking place in water solutions was affected by lunar and sunspot cycles, solar eruptions and sudden showers of cosmic rays.[8] Later Theodore Schwenk established that after an eclipse water remembered and recorded this dwindling of the light. Dr. C.W. Smith of Salford  University in Britain concluded that the smallest amounts of allergens diluted out of existence in water had transferred their properties to the dilution, but not chemically. The water in his samples had recorded the allergen's electrical impression and passed it on.[9]

At five I gave not a fig for such figuring. I was already inextricably involved with water. I understood that by its swaying inevitability water would tell me how things were. After I'd interrogated my basin, I gathered milkweed and buttercup. Singing, I stirred the blossoms in. The aroma of the petals floated up. With this flowery attention I had made the water happy. My grandmother had given me a scrap of leather, and by stretching it over a tin can, I'd made a drum. As the final act in my ceremony I sat cross legged before the basin, beating out a liquid rhythm, singing.

I didn't know that primitive cultivators believed the beating of a shaman's drum affects the structure of water. Each evening during the growing season, these first planters beat a drum beside their buckets. They stirred a bit of soil into a bucket clockwise and sang ascending notes. They stirred counter clockwise and sang a descending scale. I hadn't been told these things, and still, at dusk, when I went with my grandmother to drive the cows home, I took a jar of my magic water along, sprinkled it at the head of each row of my grandfather's corn.

Engagement with water is a sensuous affair, and we who are smitten are busy with this voluptuous doing. We recognize the erotic when we encounter it, and seek those sites where water issues from the earth: streams, springs, wells, the fountains in sunstruck plazas. Even a sprinkler's whir is ardent undercurrent. The garden hose gushes, and I drink. Drink, and offer myself to be drunk. No showers for me: I will have immersion. Immersion is the body at play—pleasure for pleasure's sake, mine and water's—the two of us tasting the slippery texture of our skins. *To be,* in my strong body, and to enter water, to push against it as it gives, to stroke myself through its slickness—this is my preferred consummation. "We could imagine disease not just a physical phenomenon," writes Thomas Moore, "but as the failure of the body to find its pleasure."[10] Swimming, I become like those ailing children dipped three times into the well of Saint Mandron, in Cornwall. Water, like a mother's kiss, makes things better.

Shoreline is a boundary. When I slide in buoyed by my element, I leave behind the body weighted down by gravity. Every time we bathe another border goes. Bits of our skin slough off like the serpent's. A morning bath re-enacts a birth: in this washing we prepare to enter the diurnal again, but as though for the first time. And if at evening, we seek the shore, it is because we long to be reborn. "From the point of view of water," Elide writes, "human life is something fragile that must periodically be engulfed, because it is the fate of all forms to be dissolved in order to reappear."[11]

Ablution echoes the annual dipping of statues of the Great Goddess. Deities, like mortals, must refurbish their vitality, and it was understood that immersion would revamp their good will and generosity. Like us, Aphrodite, Athena, and the Virgin Mary have enjoyed this ritual plunge and been revived.

A breeze rattles the palms' fringe. At dinner there is talk of a storm. I go off to my cabin, read by light of an oil lamp. Around the island, the sound of breakers flowing up over sand. Lulled by this lustrum, I fall asleep.

Later I wake in the dark: downpour batters the tin roof.

What twig dropped into what pool has thrown up this storm?

Thomas Merton said that as long as the rain spoke, he would listen. I listen, and remember there are places in the ocean that resemble a war ravaged nation. The waters record the increase of red tides, Tributyltin in the tissues of invertebrates. They record epidemics among shellfish, the bleaching and the death of corals. They register dumps of plutonium, of chlorine, of the 22.3 million barrels of petroleum spilled each year, and of the release into the deep basins of cadmium, iron, zinc, arsenic. The waters record the presence of lead in the North Sea, of nitrogen in the Mediterranean. They record, where the Mississippi empties into the Gulf, that four thousand square kilometer dead zone where there is almost no oxygen. They record the demise of salt marsh and mangrove, the disappearance of estuary, reef. They mourn the dearth of dolphin and whale, lament the deaths of seals.

The faces of those dead sea cows washed up on the North Carolina coast tell us the oceans too have their disappeared, their refugees unable to go home.

Annie Dillard writes that she would like to learn from wild animals "the dignity of living without bias or motive."[12] Water and sand do not pass judgment. Air does not present an affidavit. Fire does not assign blame. Feeling is what the elements offer us, and tonight the rain sounds like grieving. I lie back in the storm's duration, but I do not invent homilies to the effect that the vast and encompassing sweep of time will heal the waters. Instead, I imagine that time when the earth's crust, cooling, cooled enough that the falling rain did not immediately evaporate but began to collect in earth's basins. "These rains fell continuously," Rachel Carson writes, "day and night, days passing into months, into years, into centuries."[13] *Where wast thou when I laid the foundations of the earth? Who shut up the sea with doors, when it brake forth, as if it had issued out of the womb?* Like Job, I am humbled by not knowing. I listen, attendant, while the water around me has its own grieving way.

If wetness speaks of grief, it speaks also of benediction. Tonight I remember Carl, in his sixties, in the hospital where I worked as a nurse's aid. Cancer wore at him slowly, increments of change water lapping a shore. When he died and his family finished their farewells, it fell to me to prepare his body. As I washed him, I became a series of linked motions: the raising of a hand, the bowing of a head, the opening of a palm, the registration of light as it enters the retina. The stories say that to get to the other side, the dead must cross water in darkness. The water I washed Carl with was the water of that crossing, lapping the sides of the boat.

Once when I worked in a country torn by war, there came moments when the palpable despair in those around me seemed scarcely bearable. In scorching heat I went to the sea at midday, left a towel on the sand, entered the water. I swam steadily and hard, deliberate with need. I wanted to be abraded, polished like a rock turned in ocean's crucible. When I walked up the slope onto shore, my towel lay before me, a flare. I sank down and let myself drift there in the caul of exhaustion.

When I woke, the sun was low. The shore seemed scattered with yellow blossoms. Then I saw one cluster of petals skitter. As far down the strand as I could see in either direction, hundreds of tiny crabs, the bright yellow of the crayon box, had come out of hiding. They seemed bright bits of a generous wetness, an offering tossed up from the depths onto an altar. I had lain down in sanctuary. I'd awakened at the center of ten thousand prayers.

On those occasions when we feel cast out of the human world, when we want to step back from civilization and feel just how animal we really are, the natural world rises up as refuge. It is our horizon note, Elide's foundation, the bottom line. The Ancient One, life giving death bringer, is always there. She conducts her ablutions ceaselessly, and, if we join her, takes us in.

For make no mistake: our desecration of the cathedral does not mark the end of our longing for union. No nation or religion has ever put a stop to water worship, though Christians in the Middle Ages tried, beginning with the Second Council of Arles in 443, continuing until the Council of Treves in 1227.[14] Finally the church gave up. I imagine the Pope bearing the record of the Council's proceedings to the river, tearing the parchment to bits, letting these scraps fall onto the water.

For we who worship water like to give it a little something. Each time I visit a watery source, I leave a feather, a nut, a few petals, a handful of meal. When the Masai approach a river, they tear off a handful of grass, toss this offering in. We are doing what pilgrims at the lake of Saint Andeol in the Aubrac mountains did when they gave the water bits of linen, a piece of cake, a shirt or a coat. What the Trojans did, when they sacrificed live horses to their raging river. What Greek priests did, when they slaughtered oxen for the god of the sea.

Language is bodily gesture, and gesture is language. I enter the waters here one last time. Below me, the coral polyps seem a visual chorus, each uttering its note of being. I slither through this surge of oratorio, then roll onto my back, let sky see the length of me. Suddenly I'm aware of the salt in this water. Salt adds density to water's texture, and the taste, on my lips, is the taste of the body. This taste ripples through my cells, a recognition: in this vastness I am minuscule, fleshy pod inside a larger, sensing  presence.

I dive toward the grassy bottom. Kelp beds sway with the shifting current like those fields of wheat in the *Song of Songs*, and memory reverberates with my grandmother's voice. Long ago, she'd explained, the plains we walked upon were covered by water. There in my hand was the evidence, the signatures of shellfish embossed in stone.

Where is my basin now? Where those creatures whose stone imprints I found lodged in the mud of that pond? They have gone where I am going. I turn back toward shore and remember my hand reaching over my grandfather's  pool, letting the twig go, watching it fall and float on the tensile surface.Unschooled though I was in ceremony, I'd instinctively enacted  rite. My act, like the priest's, was a bodily beseeching. *Pray, offer something  alive.* In good faith I'd moved a bit of the scenery and  read the consequences of my deed in the statement of softly falling rain.

In this linked cluster of events I understood my connection to the weaving of experience we call the world. Now, beneath my feet, the bottom: water to fall into, land to stand on. Walking beside the Pacific, the Atlantic, the Indian Ocean, the Bay of Bengal, I've sometimes got down on my knees. Singer writes that she likes to image the earth as "an altar. A living one, that breathes."[15] I emerge, taller than before, and broader, my soul the shape of an unscathed sphere. I think of Rilke's ecstatic cry: *I am circling around God.* To embody transcendence is why we are here.

# Notes

1. Bonnefoy, Yves, *Mythologies*, University of Chicago Press, 1991, p. 379.
2. Singer, Natalia Rachel, *AWP Chronicle,* 1994, p.14.
3. Tall, Deborah, *From Where We Stand,* Knopf, 1993, p. 10.
4. Abram, David, *The Spell of The Sensuous,* Pantheon, 1996.
5. Elide, Mercea, *Patterns of Comparative Religion,* New American Library, 1958, p. 191.
6. Carson, Rachel, *The Sea Around Us,* Oxford, 1951, p. 9.
7. Elide, *op. cit.,* p. 192.
8. Devereux, Paul, *Earthmind,* Harper & Row, 1989, p. 176.
9. *Ibid.*
10. Moore, Thomas, *Care of the Soul,* HarperCollins, 1992, p. 164.
11. Elide, *op cit.,* p. 200.
12. Dillard, Annie, *Teaching A Stone To Talk,* Harper & Row, 1982, p. 15.
13. *Carson, op cit.,* p. 11.
14. Elide, *op cit.,* p. 194.
15. Singer, *op. cit.*

# FRUIT FLY

*Jere Odell*

Larvae under fruit skin, adults rising, ripened with yeast.
Ghosting, sometimes visible—the breath in a bowl of pears.
Bodies of ambered juice, confections for wings, eyes of candy,
      pectin for feet.
Impersonal, but at one's lips—this morning, the last to leave
      the party.
Hangers on, oblivious inebriates, clouded spirits
rimming the shot glasses & walking the wine bottles.
Sweet lover and the dew.

Or else, the object of science:  2 mm, reproducing in multiples
      x times a week.
Variables, few; traits, enough; the find, that rare recessive
      white-eyed male.
The object of science, the go-between to our genes.
Regenerative but small, the triumph of Mendel's genetics.
The fame of Thomas Hunt Morgan, the Nobel winner
      scanning his data incarnate.
& how he found his sample: Domesticity!
Left fruit on the window sill & let it swell.

Drosophilia, changeling, double soul living in the liminal:
come to the kitchen, vinegar bird, pomace fly, it's more yours
      than mine.

# POTATO BEETLE

*Jere Odell*

Scrotum-like larva, but red pastel & less pliant,
we are cousins, fleshkin of the tuber,
the starch on my breath, your nicotine pulp on my fingertips.
We also have in common: appetite—evidence ... our guts,
urge ... how we fill the earth, and (each of the other's predator)
        dreams ...
Mine: the bird to devour your strewn numbers,
a rare grosbeak, a martin tired of eating bees,
one of equal lust, like my teenage fantasies,
the voracious dream girls hawking the woods.
Yours: the Nephilim unchained, giants built to my scale,
one shoulders the sun & stinks of human touch—
that I'd never see it, but its rude hand
coming down to pinch me off this earth.

# SILVERFISH

*Jere Odell*

Bit-minnow, dull mercurial soul,
tracing the tub's false porcelain by flits,
at its tail, three aquatic hairs,
the longest could paint silk in single line,
a landscape on the king's bed sheets,
somewhere to flee, or a ship in full sail.

But where would you go?  What night
was it that put you here this morning?
Did you spring like Adam from my rug?
Did you drip, a gargoyle's breath, from my faucet?
Icarus in scales, mad artist of the void,
dragon, where do you keep your hoard?

# SESTINA FOR A POET LAUREATE

*Susan Grafeld Long*

I've heard him say *fuck*
in that creamy, softened-shoe way he pronounces words
all over this marble city:
the hushed Library of Congress, the hymnal-glue-scented
Church of the Reformation, Chapters book store,
two universities, and each time, in his voice, was a longing,

as if it were a sad but necessary thing: two bodies longing
to come together, fucking
because they wanted to try to store
within their fragile skins a memory of being alive, of new words
that float over their bed on a breeze carrying the scent
of tangerines. Tonight, people all over the city

are walking into rooms to find someone, sauntering off city
streets, just like this young man, who now sits on the rug, longing
to put his face in my dark silk skirt, which he imagines smells
of blackberries and fucking.
Nodding toward the podium, he says, *I've heard he's got a way with words.*
Then to me, *You look like you do this often. What's in store*

*for us this evening?* I sit fatigued, sipping on jasmine. From storage
rises a poem of steamy tea and morning happiness. *Any other poets in the city*
*I should hear?* he asks. My polite words
all translate into *shut-up* as the Poet Laureate reads of the longing
of angels who watch a man and a woman make love. Phlox:
I recall tall bodies moving gravely sideways toward each other, smelling

of mulched fields and river air. The poet closes and the crowd, smelling
of good wool, surges toward him. Within moments, this lantern of store
will be the center of a lonely movement of flocks
of travelers blowing like bubbles over the hills of an illustrated-Bible city.
*It is such a personal choice,* I finally answer him, longing
now for my children's bath time and reading with them nursery words.

*So,* the young man asks me, *do you have any wise words*
*for someone new like me? Any swell*
*thoughts about how to spend a Thursday night, a long*
*one?* He waves his spiral notebook at me. *I'm storing*
*up ideas for how to live in this sort of dull city.*
*By the way, is this guy political? I've heard everyone from Berkeley is fucking*

*political.* Angels watching. Men and women flocking.
A tea-fortune of words left behind on the bottom of a scented
cup.  A story.  A long city street to the car.  *What do you suggest we do now?*

*Doty. Pinsky. Hass, again. Milosz.*
I hiss.

# NATION ILL-PREPARED FOR NUCLEAR ATTACKS

*The Herald-Dispatch*, July 9, 1999

*Ace Boggess*

Being there, being afraid,
we must learn to die all over again,
like in the 50s, Red-scared &
cold with so much war that was & wasn't.
I missed that somehow, came of age
with 80s aggression & 90s ambivalence,
got hand-me-downs from parents that knew best
how to hide beneath a desk & cry.
When we reflect, we say *paranoia*,
but at least it was hand to hand & face to face,
two hesitant gladiators circling an arena
big enough to keep both separate
for years.  Now it's more like
over-the-shoulder glances, heavy breathing,
fear of dark alleys or shadows under
the bed at night.  No warnings.
Someone comes to murder us as we sleep.
Must we walk backward, cry out to see
a stranger's face, bump our heads
on walls we lacked the foresight to anticipate?
When every glass of *sauvignon blanc*
becomes a toast to nothingness,
our best crystal no longer tilts toward repose,
serenity.  I'd rather drink in peace &
let the years remake themselves,
let God reclaim fire & the last embers
of hatred it rekindles in a trembling heart.
I lack the patience to be terrified.

# SKETCH: ROOF OF THE METROPOLITAN

*Andrew Epstein*


Memorial Day 1998 we find ourselves
again we found a city with just two
central citizens we find the sculpture garden
above the park where the French girls
pull their shoulder straps down
everyone wants the best photo angle
"the top of Cleopatra's Needle, there!"
tip of stone monument
poking above the green
the French girl has a transient triangle
of red where skin's burned
"they've done a lot to this place
since I was last here"
I love how long we've been
loving how long we've been
loving each other
the crane equals construction
horizontal lines join
the couple through their shirts
people use book covers
to mask drug-store mass market
paperbacks about love and death
groups of the affluent linked
by the clink of imported beer bottles
the mind on fire
a day bursting with good news and people
as it subsides into a
pool with the rest
the subject she's been sketching
grows anxious, yawns and moves
like each minute as it nears its end
I feel that we're-on-vacation buzz
like Europe has visited our shore
the crane spells change

over the museum
I don't much like minimalism
why reduce
I'm sorry when artists die
Henry Moore, Rodin, Ellsworth Kelly's
black totem for Roy Lichtenstein,
frozen gestures of hello and love and death
I know love is evermoving
like memory not like memorials
I like the way you know a man
is European by some intangible
"perfect day" you hear crowds murmur
to one another
a communal nod and sigh in bluer air
where would we all be
without such parks and roofs
such monuments to love and death
such weather such other people

# A WEEK BEFORE OUR WEDDING I READ ABOUT THE NATIONAL SPELLING BEE WINNER

*Andrew Epstein*

From here it looks as if
the pampas will be alveolate,
though they may be merely flat.  What's
to come is as strange as a
whelp adorned with a tilak.
The days strung together before
the event like an ascending
major scale are marked
*allargando* and we
imagine everything being
redolent of hyssop
without knowing if it will be.
I feel like a Quixote
facing a blank wall soon
to be a detailed memory, or
a man who's forgotten all
he knows about cerography
just as he sits down
before the waiting wax.
Maybe my sudden parrhesia
will make this impression
as daedal as dreams
so recently created they
still seem logical.
In one week I'll be
like the practiced
chiaroscurist who wakes up to a
sudden shadowless crush of colors

# NOTHING HAPPENS AGAIN, 1978

*R.D. Skillings*

The year was almost gone. Spring was surging. April thirtieth loomed like a kind of tombstone, marking the season when birds shit copious purple from eating ivy berries, splotching steps and windshields, and the Fine Arts Work Center Fellows get ready to leave—a period naturally frenzied, sad, apprehensive, uncertain, dazed by sun after winter's bleak chill.

They had gone to the Old Colony because the Foc's'le was full of oafs and they wanted to enjoy themselves together, perhaps for a last time.

Elsie was a poet, Joanna a fiction writer, Bea and Astrid were painters. Chantel was the wife of one of the writing Fellows, a novelist herself and rejected applicant. They were embarking upon careers unlikely to provide lasting addresses. But for the moment all were at home, all had great hopes and great thirsts.

"We should have done this more often," said Joanna. "What a day!"

They marveled at the balmy weather, which brought out hibernators and hermits alike and Astrid described a guy she'd met on the meatrack whose right arm was a withered stump, result of his doctor's drunken malpractice. The guy had been grandly casual about it, gesturing with his left hand.

Astrid quoted, "I got his license, I'm going to get his house, I'm going to get his car, I'm going to get his bank account, I'm going to get everything he's got. I don't have any hard feelings. I just don't want him to have anything."

"I don't blame him," said Joanna, glancing both ways shyly over her glass, then ducking a bit to sip. "Did you read in the *Globe* about Charles Boyer's death after he sat this long vigil with his wife who was dying of cancer? He kept assuring her she was going to recover. Meanwhile he was putting off a prostate operation. He wasted away at her bedside, and then when she died he committed suicide."

"I like that one better," said Elsie.

Bea said, "My mother is demanding I come home and take care of my sick grandmother—her mother—who took care of me when she wouldn't."

"Don't do it," said Chantel.

"How can I not do it?" Bea said. "She'll just abandon her, like she abandoned me."

"I thought you were going to Yaddo," Astrid said accusingly.

"I was," Bea said.

"Yeah," Astrid said with resigned disgust.

"You only have one life," Joanna put it ruefully.

"Old age is pathetic," Elsie pursued. "A woman I know—she's probably seventy—she hired a girl to look after her ninety year old mother who's senile. The girl is about fifteen, totally innocent and terribly upset. Between changing diapers, she tries to revive the mother's mind by making her do mental exercises, like relearn the alphabet and add and subtract. The poor woman can't bring herself to disillusion the girl, but she doesn't want her mother bothered either."

"Why should it bother her?" Astrid crowed. "Hey, she's senile! She's out of it!"

"I think I'll draw the line at diapers," Bea said tartly.

"How did we get to be so morbid all of a sudden?" deplored Elsie.

"Yeah!" Joanna agreed with amazed vehemence. "We're supposed to be having a good time!"

"Have you noticed," asked Chantel, "how many people seem to be changing their names these days?"

"Who?" Astrid said. "Why?"

"A lot of people," said Chantel. She was about to theorize when Claire came in disheveled and distraught.

"I looked in the Foc's'le for you," she said. "Have you heard?"

"Heard what?" they all said warily at once.

"Eleanor Crimins got killed," Claire said. "In a car crash. She was up in Vermont borrowing her brother's van. Somebody called the office. They said you'd all gone drinking."

"So we had," Chantel murmured.

Eleanor Crimins was everybody's confidant, a wise, equable, good painter on the verge of success.

Claire sat down at the window table with them. They gaped at her in horrid shock, the dead woman's erstwhile colleagues—Elsie the intense, with square bangs and frown furrows already deeply graven between her eyes, quick to anger, quick to laugh; Irish Joanna, tall and slender, hesitant, with quavers in her voice, indignant at injustice, lately bedeviled by too many lovers; blond Bea from Pine Bluffs, Alabama, the only one in a skirt, complacent and edgy, whose secretly written novel was nearing completion; raucous, sarcastic Astrid, who smoked dope all day at her easel and dressed in thrift-shop getups; pale, sylph-like Chantel, with porcelain complexion, ash-blond hair and startling, Bay of Naples blue eyes, a withdrawn, watchful chain-smoker.

Divorced, manic-depressive Claire, in career the most advanced of them all, having two years before been a featured poet of *The Benedict Review*, had written nothing since but some fruitless notes, her interest moving toward flotsam and collage, her time gone to agonized debility or dreamy beach-combing.

"I don't know," she kept answering their one question. "I think she was on a picnic or something. The road was strewn with sandwiches and bananas and soft drinks and stuff, carrot sticks and celery, they said."

"I don't believe it!" Astrid cried, her voice flying up. "I just can't believe it. How old was she?"

"Thirty-one," Elsie said.

"Beats me by two years," said Astrid, to whom the specter of death was a daily visitant. She was the oldest of them except Claire, who was thirty-three.

Joanna said, "I don't believe it either. I can't make it seem real. I can't stand to think about it. About her, I mean."

"Is her mother still alive?" Bea asked.

Yes, yes, the others said, nodding.

"This is terrible," Elsie said. "This is the worse thing I've ever heard. Or had happen. My first friend to die."

"She was a terrific painter," Astrid said. "How could this happen?"

Two cars on the highway. Smash. What were the odds? It would never happen to you. Or anyone you knew.

Blank sorrow set in. Eyes were drenched, hugs bent till they hurt, incoherencies gnashed in their depths.

Pausing, panting, they drank.

"Well, I suppose we should...," at last said Astrid, lifting her mug. "Here's to her."

They drank.

"I have a feeling I'm not going to feel the same about life after this is over," Joanna said direly.

Chantel said, "It doesn't *get* over."

"I refuse to believe this," Bea said. "I really feel as if I could think her back to life."

"We should try," said Elsie. "All together."

Holding hands, eyes shut, they tried to bring her back to life, undo the done, presently breathed again, drank. Chantel lighted a cigarette. Astrid took one too.

"I'm getting sick to my stomach," said Claire.

"She's dead," Elsie said. "She's actually dead."

"Don't remind me," Astrid said.

"I just saw her day before yesterday," Bea said. "I walked to the Post Office with her."

Everybody but Claire, who lived off-Center, had seen her, had spoken with her, inconsequentially, the day before yesterday.

"Yeah," Astrid said. "She was feeling pretty good. She said she was over her depression."

"This is one of those really amazing things," Claire said, "that you don't want to have happen."

"God has a plan," Bea railed dully.

"No show for Eleanor," said Astrid.

"That's right!" Elsie cried. "She was going to have a show in August. In Boston."

"She can still have it," said Bea.

"Great," Astrid said with leaden irony, then, "Yeah. Well. She should. We ought to have something down here, too. At the Work Center."

For a little minute minds in accord were occupied with plans, dates, logistics.

Desolation came again. Astrid and Bea made their shrunken way to the bar with empty mugs and brought back another round.

Gone. Forever. Mangled no doubt. Food for worms or fire. Future canceled, past diminished to powerless inutility. The late Eleanor Crimins.

"I think I've got to go throw up. Excuse me," Joanna said, standing up.

Long-faced Chantel sat in silent, pale thought, chin in one hand, tall tendril of smoke rising from the other. She might have been anywhere anytime, for the calm look of her, eyes downcast like half-moons, a totem brooding.

Bea wore a scowl none of them had ever seen before. "This is not right," she said.

"Nothing's right," Elsie said.

"I know," Bea said.

"I think I sort of expected to know her all my life," Astrid marveled.

"And she was just getting going. I love her new paintings," returning Joanna said, then to their eyes, "I feel better. Not much."

"Yeah. A piece of our lives just…" Elsie opened her palms, emptied them up.

"This is horrifying," Astrid said. "I can't take it."

Mute fatality, bellies' yaw and fall, thud of tidal blood, each breath a sigh or moan.

At last Claire cried, "I can't help it—I wish I'd never told you."

They shook their heads. Not your fault, they said. Better learn like this than one by one in solitude.

Radley, heading for the Foc's'le from the West End, having penned an unprecedented thirty lines in one day, spied them in the window and went jovially in. "Witches' coven?" said he.

All looked at him with stark faces, waiting for another to speak.

"CR group?" he tried more snidely.

They looked at him with dire woe, without personal expression.

He read there some weighty kind of unwelcome, held up two fingers of his left hand, waggled them twice in blessing, backed up, and went out the door, turned by the widow, eyes averted.

"Who wants to tell anybody!" Astrid said. "He'll find out soon enough."

"Where's her boyfriend? Her ex, I guess," asked Bea. "Mr. Trouble."

"Tucson," Elsie said shortly.

"Let the office make that call," Claire said.

"He got out in the nick of time," Astrid said.

"That's right," Bea said. "He might have been with Eleanor. Be with her right now. In the morgue."

"Sleaze-ball," Elsie said.

"What d'you mean sleaze ball?" Joanna said. "He was nice. I liked him."

"You like everybody," Astrid said.

Joanna puffed out her lower lip, dropped her chin. "I guess you're right about that," she said.

Looking left and right, Joyce sauntered down the street from the East, and came in. She looked at them cheerily. "Why aren't you in the Foc's'le?" she said. "Everybody's there."

They looked at her in horrified consternation.

"Don't worry, don't worry, it's all a mistake. Somebody borrowed her brother's van. He wasn't hurt, but there was a whole family of Canadians in the other car. Three fatalities, three in the hospital. What she called to say was she wouldn't be coming back till she could find another van, but the person who took the call is a new volunteer who doesn't know anyone. I guess Eleanor was pretty upset," Joyce said.

Dumbfounded joy erupted.

"Wish I always brought such good news," said Joyce, whose gallery in town had just given her a bad slot in early June, when nothing would sell. "Feeling better, dears?" she said, and grinned wickedly.

"You can't even imagine," Astrid shouted over the laughter and tears.

"I'll bet," said Joyce, broadening her grin. "That would have made this a pretty grim day. How old was she anyway? She's having a show, isn't she? In Boston."

"Oh, I'm going to go," said Astrid, full of admonishment.

They would all be at the opening, no doubt about that, with bells on and ringing. Their voices spiraled louder and louder, laughing, crying, yelling at once, recounting what they had felt and thought, rejoicing.

Joanna's face had turned bright red; she smiled wildly, speechlessly, uncontrollably. Elsie was laughing without pause for breath, the frown lines cutting deep between her eyes. Astrid and Bea had got shots of Bushmills to help them calm down and celebrate in peace.

Claire, dazed between wonder and doubt, headed back to the Work Center, to check and re-check the truth of what had happened at a certain crossroads up in Vermont, where winter's icy writ still ran.

Joyce, who had no use for alcohol, glanced from one to another curiously, with interest fond, amused and touched, made mocking comment, wherever opening offered.

Only Chantel sat apart, silent and pale, leaning forward, chin in hand, elbow propped on crossed knee, gazing out the window at the passersby, unable to be completely glad, while their lives began to possess them again.

# TOLEDO BEND

*Simone Muench*

Green apples,
crisp as organdy.
Tangle of lips,

an embrace:
blades of wet
grass, leaves

circling in a
whirlpool of wind,
a scattering of

grackles foraging
in a lake
iridescent with scales

of bluegill,
algae's lengthy fingers.
Burst of diamonds

flung from feathers
of a pelican
as it lifts

off the water.
Hibiscus and fish
seep through

the mesh
nets we sleep
on in sunlight,

beneath mimosa's firework
flowers, sanguine as
flame; a breath

in our blood,
a crocus opening
in our throats.

# THE STUPID CLUB

*J. Morris*

Such clear eyes and careful speech.
He owned a video rental club in Duck,
North Carolina, enjoyed real death captured
on tape:

and it was astonishing how often
this happened: the Super-8 at hand to be set whirring
while your friend is eviscerated by a bear: historic records
of garrotings

filmed by patriots: and of course
the classic exploding head, found art, *de M. Zapruder.*
His taste was bad enough, but I resented his attempts
to rent me

his favorites—an oenophile
praising vintages. *Did* I want to see them?
Four years later, Kurt Cobain has . . . what is the term
policemen use?

*Sucked death? Eaten lead?* Young man with
a gun, an infant daughter, fame, money,
talent, a mother, a heroin addiction, fans
who loved him,

loved ones who didn't. Hmmmm. From this
list he selected the gun. His mother says
he often spoke of suicide. *I told him,* she says,
*not to join*

*that stupid club.* Membership in
the Stupid Club is often a big letdown
to the elected. Show us the note he left and let us
learn

what he expected. With all his wealth,
surely he bought a camcorder along the way.
Why be old-fashioned? Turn the thing on, secure it on
the tripod,

point it at your chair, walk over
and take your place. Talk. Goodbyes: sloppy
slurring fucked-head articulation. He makes a point
of telling

whomever it may concern, *Sell it,*
*I want you to, let any fan see it who wants to.*
Old red-eye winks at him. He makes eye contact, raises
the shotgun,

fits the twin barrels between
tongue and palate. The taste makes him gag.
Hurry up. An instant classic for my man
in Duck.

# A Sort of Prayer

*J. Morris*

I'm angry and waiting for snow, needing it,
a swirled and suffocating lock
slapped on the house.  Confine me,
give me silence, day upon day,
the still imprisonment, no engines,
no work, even the voices of children
who hurl themselves into the drifts
muffled and flat, the snow like death
pulling each sound deeper and destroying
echo, resonance, crystal by crystal.
I need to go deeper, hold myself quieter,
pace to and fro in a snow-socked home
as if it were my monastery.  Chanting
a liturgy I've never heard before.
Where is your blizzard, Lord, where
is that saving cold fury?  I need it
inside me; failing that, cover the sun
and stars with snow-pillows that burst,
blankets, sheets, put the entire world
to bed, and my old life to sleep
like the dog who once was faithful
but now snarls in his blindness.

# AUSENCIA IN SPANISH MEANS ABSENCE

*Virgil Suarez*

when I reach over to hold you, nothing
but air and crumpled sheets, a full pillow,
your scent gone, and I rise like a tired

dog, bones aching, mind lost to silence,
and the house creaks below my feet
on my way to the bathroom, no need

to turn on lights, to draw curtains,
when you are not here, the heat feels
charged like the warmth before a storm,

a rain might quench the thirst of flowers
outside, droopy hibiscus and gardenia;
in my dream the girls are calling for cold

water, and I go down to the kitchen,
fill a tall glass with ice and water, bring
it up to their empty beds, and here too

the flash of absence is too much, a stenciled
ivy tendril moves up the walls around doors,
through windows, grabs hold of my neck,

squeezes until I cannot breathe, scream
for everyone to come back: my dead father,
your father, grandparents, friends,

in these rooms, devoid of your presence,
your absence is like those dark, deep wells
of my childhood in Havana when I'd drop

a rock into the void, turn my ear ground-
ward, thought I could hear the voices
of the dead and gone, a plop of hope

so faint I thought I had imaged the whole
thing, like now, when I think I've merely
awakened to the sound of music, a party

in progress, the girls and you in summer
dresses, a room filled with gladioli and lilies,
everywhere color and scent, and I stand

and salute this magical reunion in humid darklight.

# HARD WORK

*Michael McCole*

We were backfilling Saturday's job, a big colonial place out in Quogue, and we were about halfway through. The dirt was mostly dark brown, black when wet, and smelled more like rot than usual. The pay was good and hourly. It was Isaac's first day. I hadn't met him before.

He was dropped off by a woman in a rattling red Ford Fairmont with one yellow door. He was wearing powder blue ski gloves and a pair of old high-top Nikes. I gave him an extra pair of work gloves, told him he should probably invest in a pair of workboots before the bottoms of his feet turned into hamburger meat, and explained to him what we had to do.

"We've got to fill all these holes in," I said. "Always get as much of the dirt back into the hole as you can. There's usually some left over, but the more you can pack in the better."

He nodded at me and picked up a shovel.

"And you've got to put the grass back in place, too, but I'll show you that when we get to it."

It was about eleven a.m. when we started. By twelve thirty I had backfilled two-and-a-half holes, and he had only just finished tamping the sod back on top of his first.

"This is some damn hard work," he said, wandering over towards me, sweating up a storm. It was the first time he had spoken to me all day long.

"Yes it is," I said. He flipped over the wheelbarrow and sat on it, taking off his gloves and drinking down half a bottle of Gatorade.

"Breaks a man's back. You're flying right along, though."

"Lots of practice," I said. "No need to kill yourself. Take it easy."

"How old are you?" he asked me.

"Nineteen."

"Nineteen!" he said. "Are you a college kid?"

"Yes I am," I said.

"Are you paying your way through?"

"My parents pay for all the college stuff. I have to work for my spending money."

"It's good of your parents to do that," he said.

"My father's been doing this sort of stuff," I said, pointing to a hole, "for years. They'd like to see me rise above it one day."

"We'd all like to rise above this," said Isaac. "Lord knows I'm trying." He looked at me and laughed. "I was nineteen once," he said. He looked up at the great blue sky and rolled his head around, cracking his neck. "I've got an interview tomorrow at a hotel. A front desk job. Health care benefits and everything, which is what I need the most. The manager goes to my church. I've got God on my side. And it would be a damn shame if I had to do this for any longer than today." He gulped at his Gatorade. "I didn't mean disrespect by that."

"It's only a summer job for me," I said.

"It's damn hard work, is what it is," he said. "But I got bills to pay."

"Yes it is."

"And me and Becca have got a little Isaac on the way. No time to be choosy."

I was leaning on my shovel and sweating. He took another sip of his Gatorade and began laughing to himself, waving at me with his hand so I would know it wasn't me he was laughing at. He took off his sneakers, picked a pebble off his left sock, dumped some sand out and into the grass, and then put them back on. The red Fairmont rattled up the road again. The woman inside stuck her head towards the passenger side window and yelled his name. "My wife," he said, and walked over towards her and the car. I cut a carpenter ant in half with the shovel's blade. They talked for a minute. She handed him something and drove off. He walked past me, back to his shovel, waving the package in the air.

"Lunch," he said, unwrapping the sandwich. He ate it in about ten seconds and got back to work.

The day became hotter as we wore deeper into the afternoon, but soon we were in the midst of clean-up. Ted, the boss, had stopped by about an hour ago to check in, but he was long gone, back to his real job. Isaac had gotten faster and was actually keeping pace with me towards the end of the backfilling, and, even better, was still full of energy for the clean-up. He was wheeling a barrowful of leftover dirt towards the back yard, to be spread beneath a cluster of cherry trees between the pool and the tennis court. The front lawn looked about as good as new. I was piling the tarps in a neat stack for Ted when a BMW pulled into the driveway. The music inside turned off and two girls, both probably a few years younger than me, stepped out.

"Wow, you filled all those holes in today?" said one of them. She was small and wearing a blue one-piece bathing suit, with a towel draped over her shoulders. Her hair was grungy with sand and ocean water. She smelled like salt and coconuts.

"There were two of us. There's another guy in back."

"Still," she said. "That was fast. You must be tired."

"What were these holes for?" asked her friend. She was wearing a Brown University tank-top over a bikini.

"They're connecting us to the water main in the street," said the first girl, looking at me. "Right?"

"Exactly," I said, smiling.

"You have dirt and stuff all over you," she said. She reached up to my face and picked a small fractal of wispy root off my cheek. Her friend rolled her eyes.

"Do you want something to drink?" she said. "I can get you some lemonade."

"That would be good," I said. "Two, actually. Isaac's in the back."

"Two lemonades," she said. The girls walked up the tiled walkway and into the house, whispering to each other.

A half minute later Isaac returned with the empty wheelbarrow.

"And that is the end of that, praise the Lord," he said. "My back is going to be angry tonight. What time is it?"

"About three," I said.

"I didn't tell Becca to come until five."

"Where do you live?" I said.

"Riverhead." Riverhead was a good half hour away and in the wrong direction.

"I'm sure they'll let you use their phone. The girl seems nice."

"The telephone company and I are in a dispute. There ain't no phone. I was hoping you could offer me a ride."

"I can give you a ride, I guess," I said. "The girl who lives here's bringing out some lemonade."

He was bending over and rubbing the sand out of his hair. "I just saw them peeking out the back windows at me," he said. He straightened back up and looked around the yard. "You can barely tell there were big holes here this morning. Ted does good work."

"We do good work."

"We *do* do good work."

The first girl, the one I assumed to be the daughter of whomever lived there, came out alone with two glasses and handed one to each of us.

"Thank you very much," said Isaac. I thanked her, too.

"We're all out of mix," she said, looking only at me. "But I found some lemons and made it freshly squeezed. Is it good?"

"Freshly squeezed?" said Isaac. He took a long sip. So did I.

"Ahhh! Just like my mamma used to make it!" he said self-mockingly, laughing, then added, "Bless her soul. This is some fine lemonade."

"Did your mother die?" asked the girl.

"My mother died a long time ago," said Isaac.

"My mother died, too," she said. "Last year. From breast cancer."

"I'm truly sorry to hear that," he said. "Just be happy that she's somewhere better now. Mine died when I was twelve. My father stabbed her."

"Oh my God," said the girl.

"Then my father stabbed himself, and he died, too," said Isaac. "Right after he stabbed me."

We were in my truck, pulling onto Sunrise Highway when Isaac said, "You know I made all that up. About my daddy killing my mother. That never happened."

"Are you serious?"

"My father died in Vietnam. My mother lives in Bridgehampton. That lemonade girl lives there in her nice big house in Quogue with her BMW. She doesn't know my sort of thing. It's a shame that her mamma died, but she needed a little shaking up. Make her consider things she normally wouldn't. Any girl that grows up with a tennis court in her back yard…"

"I was going to ask her for her number. You ruined it."

"You don't want anything to do with her," he said. He looked at me. "You can get her number from Ted," he added.

"It's not the same."

"I could tell that she thought she liked you," he said. "She would've given it to you."

"She thought she liked me? What is that supposed to mean?"

"Well, you might be what she thinks she likes right now, but you ain't. You would be someone she could show to all her friends, her sweaty ditch-digging boy, but then when she realized that you can't offer her anything beyond that, she'll kiss your damn ditch-digging ass good-bye."

There was silence for a moment as I worked over what he had said. "You are a wacked-out dude," I finally blurted.

"You can say whatever you want to me," he said. "I know who I am. You're too young to know who you are." He picked a chunk of mud off his jeans and threw it out the open window. "It would be easy for me to make you feel this small," he said, squeezing a centimeter of air between his

126

fingers. "You know that, too. Why don't you come to church with me and Becca on Sunday?"

I had no idea what to say.

"I only ask you because I like you and think we could be of some use."

"You are a wacked-out dude," I said.

"I am what I am."

We drove most of the rest of the way in silence. He lived in a rough part of Riverhead, which wasn't unexpected. His place was a tiny yellow two-story with a rickety chain-link fence around the front. A sign, faked to look like a license plate, was wired into the fence. It said *Beware of God*. There was a little swatch of a lawn, and a birdbath. It was one of the more obviously cared-for properties on the block. When he got out he asked me to say a lucky prayer for him over that hotel job, and I told him I would. On the way home I stopped at the house in Quogue again, under some bogus pretext, and got the girl's phone number. She asked me to come in, said that she would make sandwiches, but I was covered with too much dirt, so I declined. Her name was Sloan and she was going to Wellesley in a couple months to begin her college career. We talked briefly about our families, then I told her I'd call her soon, hopped in the truck and drove away.

A couple nights later Ted called me with a job in Westhampton Beach. He asked me if I could pick Isaac up beforehand. He said that he would pay me a few extra bucks for it. I swung by Isaac's place, grabbed him, and headed south. He had a new pair of leather gloves, but was still wearing the sneakers. His T-shirt said, *Born Again. Hallelujah.*

"Did you get the job?" I asked.

"They asked me back for another interview," he said. "This time I'm talking to some regional person. I want the job, you know, but it is only a hotel desk job. I'm not applying for the FBI with all these damn interviews." He laughed. "But I'll get it," he said, and then he made a crazy man face. "I can see into the future."

"Don't do that," I said, laughing.

"Today we're digging down instead of filling in, right?"

"Hallelujah."

"Hallelujah," he said. "And my back still hurts from Tuesday. Hallelujah."

"After today," I said to him, "everything is going to hurt."

"I know, I know...," he said. "Digging down. Westhampton."

We got to the job and it was surprisingly small. There were only four holes to drop and, being Westhampton, it was sure to be sand all the way.

After laying out our tarps we started cutting the grass into neat little rect-
angles. I stopped for a moment, looked at Isaac and said, "I went back to
that job in Quogue and got the girl's phone number."

"You fool," said Isaac, lifting a rectangle of thick grass off the ground
with his square shovel, exactly as I had just shown him how to do it.

"We went out last night."

"The blind leading the blind," he said. "How'd it go?"

"Strange," I said.

"I'm not surprised," tossing the square shovel aside and grabbing the
long handled one. He kept his head lowered towards the beginnings of his
hole and started digging, so I stopped talking.

It was about seven a.m., and the normal early morning South Shore fog
was beginning to burn off. You could feel the temperature rising against
your skin. We were working in silence for about a half hour when I finally
said, "You know what she did?"

"No idea," he said, as if the conversation had never halted. "But I bet I
can guess."

"Then what?" I said.

"You went out and met some of her rich friends," he said, looking at
me. "And she embarrassed you." He was smiling. "Said something stupid.
Forgot who you were."

"No, not at all," I said. "We went out alone. That part was fine, I guess.
It's what she said before that."

"So what did she say?" he said.

"I don't even feel like I can tell you."

"Suit yourself," he said.

"Well," I said. "She like…" I leaned on my shovel and looked at him.
"You understand that this is the first time we went out, right? But as soon as
we got into the truck—we were going out to John Scott's on Dune Road—
right away she tells me that isn't it so annoying that people have to go out
on dates, because all she wants to do is for me to screw her brains out.
We had hardly even said hello. Maybe there's something wrong with
me, but…."

Isaac was laughing. "So what did you say?" he said.

"I didn't say anything. I was freaked out."

"Doesn't surprise me," he said.

"Surprised me. And get this—and I swear to God that this is true. But
she reaches inside her shirt and takes her bra off. Pulls it out her sleeve. You
know how girls do that. And she says, 'My father is away on business and
you're going to screw my brains out tonight.'"

I shook my head and spit absentmindedly into the hole I was digging. "I can't believe I'm telling this to a guy with a Born Again Hallelujah shirt."

"Don't mind this old rag," he said.

"Yeah," I said. "The weirdest thing was that once we got to John Scott's she starts behaving perfectly normal. Like the car ride never happened. I don't know, man. It was weird. And all I could think about was that this girl's purple lace bra is laying across my dashboard right now and how good looking she is and that I could have her any moment I want. I could barely talk through dinner."

"It sounds to me like you have some issues to resolve with yourself," he said. "Sounds to me like you don't know what you want."

"I can't figure it out," I said. "We're going out again tomorrow night." He stopped digging and looked at me. "You damn kids are like a bunch of rabbits," he said, laughing and shaking his head. "Give her my best, that rich little thing. Must be nice to think you have not a care in the world. Seventeen years old. Damn."

The sand was coming up like sugar. Digging was almost a pleasure. I kept assuring Isaac that it was the best he would ever see, and he kept assuring me this was the last he'd ever see, soon as he got that hotel job. We got deep into our holes, tired, alone and determined, and struck the water table. The final half foot or so soaked through my boots and into my socks. I tossed my shovel to the side, hiked myself out, and sat down on the front steps of the house with my water bottle in my hands. Isaac was not yet done with his hole, down in the ground a little bit below shoulder-deep, which meant he had about a half foot to go.

He was bringing up the wet sand now, too, but he was twisting himself around like a contortionist, trying desperately to get the angles of his body and limbs and the long shovel all working together. Every once in a while it worked, and his face would relax with relief, but, more often than not, he would manage only to bump the butt-end of the shaft on the edge of the hole, knocking the dirt off the blade and watching it plop back to the bottom, or he would successfully get the blade out of the hole, but not at a flat enough angle and the dirt would slide away before he got it to the tarp or, most frustrating of all, he wouldn't even be able to get the shovel leveled out enough at the bottom. When this happened, the sand would just wait there while his shovel came up clean and wet. I started to laugh.

"How y'all do this?" he asked.

"Practice."

"You and your damn practice," he said. "My socks are getting soaked."

"I'll finish that one up for you in a little while," I said. "Get on out and take a break. You're killing yourself."

"I ain't killing myself. I'm making myself stronger," he said, climbing clumsily out of the hole and rolling over onto his back. He took his shirt off and laid there in the grass. There was a big, dark scar on the left side of his chest. "Ahhh," he said. "Now this is nice."

"I didn't sleep with Sloan," I said.

"No kidding," he said.

"I freaked out. I choked," I said. "She told me she was a virgin, and— I just dropped her off and went home."

"You did the right thing," he said.

"It didn't feel like the right thing," I said. "It felt like the chump thing."

"Just because you didn't bust your move doesn't mean you're not a man," said Isaac, staring up at the clouds. "No matter what she thinks. What it does mean is that you're a gentleman."

"I still feel like a chump," I said. "A schmuck."

He laughed. "You think you got problems?" he said. "Someday you'll realize that that problem is a whole lot of nothing—that most problems are a whole lot of nothing. One day you'll realize that the only true problems there are is if your woman is with someone else, if you've got something bad like cancer, or if you've got far too many bills then you can pay. Luckily for me I'm only suffering from one of those problems right now. That and blisters on my feet."

"That doesn't help me much today," I said. "Are you going to tell me what that scar is on your chest?"

He hesitated for a moment, then said, "That's something you're going to continue to know nothing about."

I finished Isaac's hole for him while he started on a new one, the one closest to the house. He was digging in a spot that had already been dug up once before, probably when the place was built. He was pulling all kinds of crap out of the ground, everything from old beer bottles to a padlock to a rotted-out transistor radio. But about three feet down he hit something solid and metal. I could hear him banging away on it and complaining.

"No!" I shouted. "It might be a well."

"Looks like a car to me," he said. He banged on it with the shovel again.

"Stop!" I said.

"I'm telling you it's a car," he said. I climbed out of my hole and was standing above him. He bent over and pulled up a hood ornament. "See," he said. "It's a Pontiac."

"Jesus," I said.

"Who the hell put a damned car in my hole?" he said. "And a Pontiac. The same car my father used to drive."

"You're standing on the hood," I said.

"What kind of a person buries a car?" he said.

"This means that we're going to have to dig another hole," I said.

"Let's dig it up," he said, looking towards me, squinting in the sun. "Maybe there's a body in it."

"We have to dig around it. We have to dig a new hole."

"Maybe there's a treasure in the trunk. Maybe the horn still works."

"Ted's going to freak when he sees this. The people who live here probably don't even know they have anything buried in their front yard."

Isaac was hacking away at the north wall of his hole with the blade of the shovel. "I'm going to find the windshield," he said. "I'm going to find the body inside. There can be anything in this car. Anything." He bent over into the hole and shouted towards the wall. "Mr. Hoffa! Can you hear me, Mr. Hoffa? Are you in there, sir? Hold on a minute, sir. We'll be there shortly!"

Eventually I finished my hole and helped Isaac finish the new one he had to start. There was nothing extraordinary pulled from the depths of this one besides a bunch of corroded D-cell batteries and a toothbrush. We threw hunks of plywood over the holes so no animals or kids would fall in, and I scribbled a quick note to Ted on a napkin from my glove compartment. I put it on one of the pieces of plywood and we used the hood ornament and a rock as paperweights. It was about 1:30 p.m. when we rolled out of town. Ted would come by after work with another guy, Howard, and tunnel underground from hole to hole with an air compressor, and then pull the copper piping through from the house's basement to the last hole by the street.

I drove Isaac home to Riverhead and wished him luck on his next interview. He said thanks, adding that he thought that his feet were bleeding, and that maybe he'd see me once again some day.

A few mornings later, on Saturday, I awoke in a panic in Sloan's bedroom, frantically searching for the time. Her father was once again gone for the weekend and she had thrown a giant, blurry bash. I immediately recalled a nasty argument between the two of us—something to do with her friends—and then there I was waking up in her bed wearing nothing but my socks. It was 4:43 a.m. I had to be at work in a little over two hours, ready to dig. I jumped up, still drunk, and apologized. I kissed her good-bye and ran out to the truck. I was home in record time, got in the shower to sober up, dried off, put on a dirty pair of jeans and a T-shirt, my boots, chugged about a gallon of water and orange juice, took two aspirin, said hello to my father who had wandered out of his bedroom to go to the bathroom, and dazedly climbed into the truck and headed down the road towards Sunrise Highway.

I drove through the fog to the house in Remsenberg where Ted had told me to be, and was actually the first one there, but feeling like I was going to die. The house was about ninety feet removed from the road. It was a decent-sized job. I felt horrendous, so I sat on the front yard and stared at the grass.

Five minutes later Ted appeared. "You're here bright and early," he said. I stood up and helped him unload his truck. A couple minutes after that Howard pulled his van to the side of the road and climbed out. "Gentlemen," he said, and started pulling tools from the back.

"Are you sick or something?" said Ted to me. "Oh…I see. Tsk, tsk…. Howard! Billy's hungover. He doesn't look like he's going to be able to work. Should we fire him?"

"Yep," said Howard.

"You're fired," said Ted.

"Really?" I said.

"What do you think?" said Ted.

"You and the horse you rode in on," said Howard.

"Am I really fired?" I said.

"No," said Ted.

"Yes," said Howard, still across the street, his ass and legs dangling from the back of his van with a clanking and scraping of metal and sand.

"How's about this?" said Ted. "You work as best you can this morning. If you are useless, you go home and I won't pay you for being here today. If you are more than useless, keep working. Isaac's working today, too, so we can get by without you. But if you go home this is strike one. And you only get two strikes. We've got three jobs. This is the biggest one, though. We'd survive without you."

"I'm all right," I said. "I'll stick it out."

"Good answer," said Ted. "A little work will do you good."

"You're too easy on him," said Howard. "Not only should we can him but we should tell his father why." He was smiling, walking towards us with a couple shovels in his hands, so I gave him the finger and he laughed.

"You see that?" he said to Ted, still laughing. "The kid's got no respect. Do I have to take that from him? What would his old man think?"

The ground was like concrete. The grass came up fine, but everything beneath the topsoil was solid. Ted had to pull the jackhammer off the back of the truck, attach it to the air compressor, and rattle the neighborhood's brains out before eight a.m. The noise split my head in two. I still felt horrible and I was sweating like a meatloaf. Ted and Howard were making fun of me, but then the conversation shifted.

"Where's Isaac?" said Ted.

"Am I his babysitter?" asked Howard.

"He's a half-hour late," said Ted.

"Do you know about the hotel thing?" I asked them. They didn't, so I told them.

"It was nice enough of him to call me and tell me," said Ted afterwards, annoyed.

"I'm OK," I said. "I'll work the day. You don't need him."

"That's not the point."

"I told you not to hire him," said Howard.

"This ground is horrendous," I said.

"The guy's got to be closet nutcase with what happened to him, and he *is* a Jesus freak," said Howard. "I feel for him, and I've got nothing against Jesus, but you can't rely on guys like that. The last black guy you had working for you, remember him?"

"I'm happy for him. I'm glad he got that job," I said. "He said he needed the health insurance. I'm glad he got it. He hated digging."

"His wife is pregnant," said Ted.

"Doesn't excuse him from not calling," said Howard.

"Did he tell you about his mother and father?" Ted asked me.

"No," I said, wiping sweat off my face with my arm and holding my breath to combat a quick rush of nausea that had just come on. It passed without incident.

"When he was a kid his father killed his mother. Stabbed her about twenty times in the chest."

"He told that to the girl who lived in that big colonial place out in Quogue," I said. "But then later he told me he was just kidding."

"The girl that you're screwing?" asked Ted. He turned to Howard, said, "I hear everything, don't I, Howard? I hear every little detail. Billy hasn't learned yet how much the neighbors talk. Now what would his old man think about *that?*"

They both laughed.

"And I bet you that's where you were last night," said Howard. "Getting drunk and lucky with the homeowners' daughters. Sounds like me in my young days."

"I think we got in a big fight last night," I said.

"You think?" said Ted. "Must've been some night."

"Women," said Howard. "You can't live with them, you can't kill them." We both looked at him.

"So that's true then? About Isaac?" I asked.

"It's true," said Ted.

"Did his father stab Isaac too, then?"

"Yeah," said Ted. "He stabbed the mom about twenty times, stabbed Isaac, then stabbed himself in the throat. Cut his own throat out."

"I remember," said Howard. "Goddamned wacko. He was a crackhead, they said. Just freaked out."

"Isaac's still got the scar on his chest," said Ted. "He showed it to me a few months ago. Before I hired him. It's a nasty, scary looking thing. That story was big news back in the day. Ask your dad. He'll remember."

"How do you know him?" I said. "Isaac?"

"His wife cleans my sister-in-law's house."

"I wonder why he told me that he made it up," I said. "He's a Born Again, you know. You figure he'd be more…openhearted."

"Yeah, well, that's not the type of thing you want to advertise," said Ted. "It is good that he got that job, though. He could've called, but I'm happy for him. Health insurance is important when you've got a kid coming."

"This ground," Howard said. "It's like concrete."

Ted started up the compressor again and hit the holes another time with the jackhammer, once again splitting the ground, the air, and my hangover into jagged fragments. The morning haze had evaporated and the sky was a big blue sheet. We three got back to digging. I still felt sick. I remembered seeing guys doing things like this when I was a kid—digging holes, using jackhammers, getting dirty—thinking that they were maybe the luckiest men in the world. Howard was twice as fast as the rest of us. He could dig like a bulldozer, but not on that day. Not with that ground. You had to use your shovel more like an axe on ground like that, and that's exactly what he was doing—chopping away at the solid stuff, hoping to find a soft spot somewhere underneath. Ted had unlimited energy at all times, but he was short and not stocky, which isn't the easiest thing to overcome when tossing your weight around is essential to success. He was a firm believer in the jackhammer in such situations, although Howard and I tended to take the ground as a challenge. Of course, we never complained when Ted broke up the ground for us, but we never asked for it, either. Our silent competition wouldn't allow it. I looked up at the circling seagulls and then heard that familiar red and yellow rattling as the Ford Fairmont sidled up to the edge of the road.

He climbed out of the car and walked towards us without a word. He was wearing a pair of jeans, a sleeveless T-shirt, brand new workboots, and the same leather gloves as last time. He turned back towards the car, as if he had remembered something to say, but it was already clamoring off so he made his way towards us.

"I'm sorry I'm late, Ted," he said. "Family things. Hello, Howard. Billy."

"Hi," said Howard.

"No sweat," said Ted.

"How's your girl, Billy?" he said, not even looking at me, walking past us and towards the pile of tools.

"I think we got in a fight," I said.

He picked up a shovel and pointed to a spot on the grass that Ted had spray-painted, marking out where a hole was going to have to be dug.

"Dig here?" he said.

"The ground's like concrete," said Howard. "It's horrible, spiteful shit."

"Cut the grass out and I'll hit it with the jackhammer," said Ted.

"No need," said Isaac. We watched him lay out a tarp and kept watching as he cut out the grass with a square shovel. When he was through he picked up a long-handled shovel and applied his weight to it, trying to force the blade into the ground. It didn't drop more than a half inch. "Damn, this mother's tough," he said, scrunching up his face. "Come on, you bastard." The muscles in his shoulders and neck knotted as he maneuvered the shovel around, searching for a better angle of attack. He was making a tiny bit of progress, but still not progress worthy of his effort. He started stomping up and down. The blade hardly seemed to budge, but after a few seconds it was somehow most of the way into the ground. He put some weight on the shovel's shaft. The blade stood firm where he had worked it in, and we watched the shaft creak and bow as he bent it down, waiting for the wood to explode into splinters at any moment. "Come on, you!" he said. I couldn't believe how hard that ground was. He let go of the shovel and looked up at us. The shovel's shaft vibrated in the sun.

"Don't sweat it," said Ted. "Just let me hit it with the jackhammer. No need to kill yourself."

Isaac's forehead was already covered with beads of sweat. "I ain't killing nothing," he said. "I'm just trying to dig this hole out for you." He put some weight on the shovel's shaft again and bent it back down. We held our breaths, waiting for the splinters to begin flying. "You know I've got too many goddamned bills," said Isaac. "Getting jerked around by that damned hotel. And Thursday night Becca goes into the hospital, comes out, and she ain't even pregnant anymore." He let the shovel relax for a moment as he readjusted his angle of attack. "Got us a dead baby boy smaller then a fist. They said there's something wrong with my wife's insides and he just didn't want to be in there." He put some weight onto the shovel again, the shaft bowed, and then the dirt above the blade actually began to crumble while the shaft moved towards the ground. "Anyway, there ain't going to be any little Isaacs. Not now, not never. We buried our only shot yesterday."

"I'm sorry," said Ted.

"That's all right," said Isaac, dumping the shovelful onto the tarp. "Wasn't anything you did. Life goes on, I suppose." He stopped and looked at the patch of dirt below him.

"'I'd appreciate it if you did get this with the jackhammer," he said. "You were right. This is some hard, hard earth."

Ted walked off towards the truck.

"You can take the day, Isaac," Howard said. "You don't have to be here. I'm sure Ted will let you go."

Isaac smiled at him, said, "I've got to be here. I've got to pay my bills. And I already bought the boots." He lifted a foot up into the air and displayed it for Howard. "And what else would I do with my day? Sit around and think too much?"

Isaac turned towards me and smiled. I wanted to say something, but couldn't come up with anything worthy. My brain was pulsating behind my eyeballs.

Isaac worked the entire day. I made it, too, although the hangover never quite gave up on me. The four of us had worked quietly and seriously. Nobody laughed. We only spoke about job things—about pipe and shovels and dirt and sand. We finished a couple of hours early, too, standing around, looking at each other, surprised at our efficiency.

"I'll take Isaac home today," said Ted to me. "Go get some sleep. You did a great job." He patted me on the shoulder, picked up a couple folded tarps, and carried them off towards his truck. I turned to Isaac.

"So you and your girl got into a fight," he said to me.

"I think so," I said.

"It doesn't surprise me much," he said, taking his gloves off and tiredly stuffing them into his back pocket. "About what?"

"I don't remember."

Isaac laughed. "Are you going to go to her?"

"I'm going home," I said. "I'm exhausted. I'm going to take a shower, eat mom's cooking, and sleep."

"Suit yourself," said Isaac. "But I know that you're a better man than that, Billy." Then he gave me his phone number for backfilling day—his phone had just been reactivated—and said good-bye. He climbed into Ted's truck and they drove off.

I parked my truck on the curb, rubbed off as much dirt from my clothes as I could, tramped up the long walkway that ran parallel to the holes that Isaac and I had backfilled on the day we met, and rang her doorbell. She answered the door in a pair of cut-off shorts and a T-shirt. She squinted in the sunlight, and frowned slightly.

"Hi," I said.

"Hello," she answered, quietly, not looking me in the eye.

"Did we get in a fight last night?" I asked her.

"Yes," she said.

"About what?" I asked.

"I don't want to talk about it," she said.

I was embarrassed. "Can I come in?" I asked.

It's always jarring to see the residue of a party, the day after, when all the guests have vanished and the grime has had time to set in. The parts of the house that she hadn't yet cleaned were a mess. The parts that she had already taken care of were perfect.

"Do you need any help?" I asked.

She sighed. "Help me move the refrigerator," she said. "Something spilled behind it."

We went on like that for another two hours or so, conquering the grime with Windex and paper towels, Pledge and Love My Carpet, her house slowly becoming the shining castle it had been before the previous night's guests arrived. My arms were more tired, it seemed, by scrubbing countertops and tiles than they were from tackling the half-dozen holes that I'd dropped earlier. The sun was now low in the sky, and the light was pouring directly through the windows, its rays almost parallel to the floor.

The glass tables were dazzling in the front room, and rainbows were reflecting through the crystal flower vases by the big bay windows.

I walked into the pantry with a bag full of garbage.

"I found a bunch of bottlecaps in the couch," I said.

"We still have to clean the kitchen floor," she said.

I didn't even see Sloan for the last half hour or so. When I finally finished scrubbing down the patio table in the back yard, I went back into the house to look for her. She was sitting on her bed upstairs, her knees pulled up towards her chin.

"I'm sorry," she said, when I walked into the room.

"About what?" I asked.

"Last night," she said, looking at the rug near her feet. "And for making you clean. I didn't mean for you to come here."

"I wanted to come here," I said. "I'm happy to help."

"I don't want to go to college," she said. "I don't want to leave here."

I didn't know what to say. I picked up a stuffed animal from her dresser, then put it back down again. I looked at her. She was still looking at the rug. "Can you please leave me alone for a minute?" she asked. "I'm sorry. I just need to be left alone."

The entire house was shimmering with order. Everything was scrubbed, scoured, and washed. The air smelled antiseptic. The walls felt like silk. The only dirty thing in the house was me. I found Isaac's phone number in my wallet. I dialed the numbers. Becca answered.

"Hello?" she said.

I hesitated for a moment, but feeling foolish, I blurted out, "Hi."

"Hi," she said. "Who is this?"

I didn't say anything. Everything I could think of felt so stupid and small. I felt insignificant and ridiculous. I didn't know why I even called.

"Hello?" she said again.

I hung up the phone.

I walked to the rear of the house, opened the sliding doors, and stepped outside. It was humid. Sunset was about half an hour away, and the sun was just beginning its heavy assault on the horizon. The tennis courts were off to the right. The pool was on the left. Straight ahead was an empty birdbath, and then beyond that was a small group of three or four fruit trees. I turned around and looked at the house behind me. Something flickered in one of the upstairs windows. Sloan was staring down. As soon as I noticed her, she ducked away and disappeared.

I walked towards the trees. The hangover was reasserting itself. It was getting late and I hadn't eaten in hours. I was dehydrated, too. There was an empty bottle of Champagne laying in the grass. I picked it up. It was cheap champagne—the kind that comes in a green bottle. It was a bottle that I'd brought. It was my contribution to the party. Sloan and I drank it with a couple of her friends, right there beneath the cherry trees, while the rest of the party carried on inside. I remembered that when we went back in, Sloan popped the cork on another bottle of Champagne. It was from her father's liquor cabinet. She told me how much her father paid for it, how it was imported exclusively to a store in East Hampton that he visited regularly. I asked her if she would get in trouble for drinking it. She told me that he wouldn't care. She said that it was the best Champagne in the world and that he liked her to indulge in the finer things, that he had taught her to tell the difference between the good stuff and the cheap stuff solely by taste, and that her father would be proud that she knew enough to open it. She tipped the bottle back and swallowed. "It's so good!" she said. "Try!"

I flipped out. I accused her of making fun of the Champagne that I'd brought. I called her a rich brat. A bunch of her friends got in my face. They told me to go back to my white trash town. I called them a bunch of pompous, sissy assholes. I told them that I could beat them all up. Sloan screamed at me that I had no class, no manners. I remember storming outside, to the back yard, right where I was standing. I remember being infuriated. I remember her coming out and me pushing her away. Somehow, though, I still wound up with her that night.

I threw the bottle over the fence that separated her yard from a scrubby mess of bushes, needles, and shrubs. I heard it land with a thud and a tinkle on the other side. I turned around, walked through the house, out the front door, got into my truck, and drove away.

Twenty minutes later I opened the chain-link gate in Riverhead, the gate shrilly swiveling on its hinges, and walked up the short path to the front door. I knocked. Becca answered.

She seemed exhausted as well. She was wearing a lime green dress and had a towel in her hands.

"Hello," I said. "Is Isaac here?"

"You're one of Ted's workers," she said. "Aren't you Billy?"

"Yes," I said. "That's me."

"I've heard so much about you. Please come in."

The inside of the house was bright and cheerfully decorated. Most of the furniture was disintegrating. The rug looked as if it was thirty years old.

But the small touches were charming. The lamp shades were all brightly colored. The photographs on the wall were of beach scenes and picnics with blue skies. The people in the pictures were always smiling. And the windows were all opened wide, flooding the inside of the house with the last remaining light of the day. Isaac was sitting on the couch in the front room, in shorts and a T-shirt, reading an auto magazine.

"Hello Billy," he said.

"Hey," I said.

He was looking at me, smiling. Becca was standing off to the side, smiling as well.

"You're the only white person we've had in this place in about two years who don't work for a utility," said Isaac. He laughed. Becca blushed. I stood there stupidly, knotting my hands before me.

"I wanted to come and say that I was sorry," I said. "I felt bad that I didn't say anything to you all day."

"That's all right," said Isaac. "I understand you were not your usual sharp self."

"Please, sit down," said Becca.

"I'm dirty," I said.

"Don't mind that old couch," said Isaac. "Take a seat. Make yourself at home."

I sat.

"Where are you coming from?" said Isaac. "Did you stop by your girl's house like I told you to?"

"Unfortunately," I said.

"Is it better that I don't ask questions about it?" he said.

"Probably," I said. "I helped her clean. I just left."

"You don't look so good," said Isaac. "Do you want something to eat. Are you thirsty?"

"Could I have a glass of water?" I said.

"Of course," said Isaac. "Becca, get Billy a glass of water." She smiled, stood, and walked into the kitchen.

"Ted told me that he told you about what happened with my parents," said Isaac. "I want to apologize to you about that. I should have told you the truth."

"You did at first," I said.

"It's not the type of thing I want to flaunt around," he said. "I hope you understand. It does the world no good by me dredging it up again and again."

"I understand," I said.

"I hoped you would," he said.

Becca returned with a pitcher of water, three glasses, and a bowl of Saltines. I drank my entire glass in one long gulp. Isaac's eyebrows climbed his forehead.

"Billy looks thirsty," he said to Becca.

"Have some crackers," she said to me.

"You look terrible," Isaac said to me.

"I'm on about two hours of sleep," I said. I picked up a Saltine and ate it. "I love your lamp shades. Did you make them?"

Becca didn't answer, but smiled.

"Why don't you take a nap?" said Isaac. "We've got the back room. Can we put him in the back room, Becca?"

"You can lay down back there for a little while," said Becca. "You shouldn't drive home as tired as you are."

"I'm still in my work clothes," I said.

"Oh! I forgot to tell you," said Isaac, "I got a job interview on Monday with a sailboat company."

"Really?" I said. "That's great."

"They run from the mouth of the Peconic, into the bay, then out into the ocean. They go up to Block Island, Newport, up the river to Providence. Three- or four-day trips. All those places. They take people out on tours and teach them to sail."

"I didn't know you knew how to sail," I said.

"I learned when I was in the Navy," said Isaac. "Italy."

"I hadn't known you were in the Navy."

"There's lots you don't know," he said. "I figured you'd have figured that out by now. Next summer, you can come work for me. You can be my deck swabber."

"Don't you listen to him when he gets like that," said Becca to me. "You know he's just playing with you."

Isaac laughed. I smiled at the both of them.

"You look like you need a nap," said Isaac. "You're taking a nap. I'm not going to be held responsible when you drive off the road and twist yourself around a telephone pole. What would Ted do then? He'd fire my black ass."

"I really should go home," I said.

Isaac nodded to Becca. "Nonsense," she said. "Come with me."

The back room was the dead baby's room. There was a second-hand crib nestled into a corner. A crucifix was fastened to the wall above the short end of the crib. On the wall above the long side was a cartoon of the animals filing onto Noah's Ark. Above the crib hung a mobile of slowly rotating plastic stars and moons. There was a small mattress in the other corner of the room. Becca covered the mattress with a blanket and handed me a pillow. "Don't worry about anything," she said. "Get some sleep." She smiled and left.

I laid down on the bed. I knew I could fall asleep in seconds. But then Isaac's silhouette appeared in the doorway. He looked at me for a small moment, and then began to close the door as quietly as he could.

"Isaac," I said.

The door opened slowly, a small wedge of light expanding in the dusty air.

"I am really sorry," I said. "I feel terrible about everything."

"I appreciate it, Billy," he said. "We've just got to keep moving."

"You were right about Sloan."

"Everybody's got to learn the hard way," he said. "There's nothing in this world that ain't hard work. But don't say I didn't warn you." He laughed. "I'm just kidding. Get some sleep, Billy. I'll call your folks for you. I'll tell them where you are."

"Yes," I said. "Sleep." I was already halfway out. I was so comfortable. I heard him close the door and the darkness flooded me.

# NO PLACE LIKE HOME

*Robert Hahn*

Centuries pass and no one passes through
The town, a famous stop on the great route

West. Not now. The motel is boarded up.
Gas-stations. Pawn shops. Though a used book store

Seems odd. Inside it's chaos. Paperbacks
Of new age faith and deadly crime-sprees stacked

Beside dime novels and penny dreadfuls—
We browse through the junk, looking for treasure—

But why here? From behind his heaped ash-tray
And smudged ledgers—a fanatic?—he waves

The thought away: "Just helping my wife—I'm
Retired, Marines—it's *her* bright idea."

Hey, it's a great idea, though who reads
Anymore. Outside the street is empty,

Sun-shocked. Reptile-black shadows. Killers crouch
in sunken grease pits, aching to get out

                    of their time
                              of Kansas


                                             of Council Grove.
The town lay near the river, a willow and cedar oasis
                              for prairie schooners
a long file of bleached clouds along
                    the trace of trade
                              heading out

from Council Grove        the last stop      to retool and repair

axle, hub, spoke, and rim
               back on the road
back in motion        as the rolling grass      closed over behind you

                                        Coronado

camped near the grove in 1540
                              amazed

     accounts of the time relying heavily on the same phrase
     in arias, at the top of each rise

                    as far as the eye can see
                                        it was vast


                                   but it was not
the ecstatic
                    they came for,
with maps to complete      commissions      to finish,
they were travelling on business, we have their accounts

if not of the Cherokee, whose lands these were,
     whose accounts were burned in later      as policy
          down the chain of command
                                   along the Santa Fe trail

                                        Kit Carson

exterminating brutes
                    clouds a mirror
                    of herds below, "we shot
                    as many as we wished"

from every hill it flowed away
                              over rock

over the limestone

        skull which was there
   before they were thought of, before
      there was thought

in flint outcrops

                          in empty days
not yet known as empty
             or as days

no clouds    a pure    infusion of light.
no word           and no one
               to say it to  or to see

how high the sun    how dark
   they are, in profile,    the pterodactyls

      taking long views    down  to their prey

feeling  no awe    or wish
   for release    no rage   only this

attention and descent
   in off-beat   pauses   pulses  dust-stir and wing-soar
     from the cliff-edge

          sail shadows rushing up
on the inland sea   on its dried floor
  ripples incised in stone, cross-hatched eras
      to be named later

of intrusions folding layers
   back on themselves, into risen hills
silted with dust and  coated
     with flowing grass
       as far as the eye could see

In what would be home, for ten thousand years,
To the Mound Builders and Forest Dwellers

And eight tribes including the Kansa, the name
Placed on a map by Marquette, to claim it

For France—a wilderness, crossed by Vial
On what would become The Santa Fe Trail—

*Kansas.* "Bleeding Kansas," in the dark days
Of the 1850's, when Pro-Slavers

Burned the town of Lawrence, whereon John Brown
Knelt by the Pottowatamie and found

Vengeance was his, in the name of the Lord,
Killing two sons of James Doyle with a sword,

Then Doyle, with a pistol, at point-blank range,
A bright, deafening roar of revelation.

# ORUS, THE FALLEN ANGEL: AFTER DALI'S
## *ATAVISTIC VESTIGES AFTER THE RAIN*

*Ryan G. Van Cleave*


Even God has a hole through his heart, an impurity like the
    interworked spirals
that are the flesh of sky, the interlacing of bright worn smooth by
    years of overuse.

With his son by the hand, the man points at the dark brook before
    them, the water
deep and fast-moving with the faces of their dead like memory-
    photographs

that cannot be destroyed; symphonic the horizon, how the light
    shines even when
we are gone, its elaborate copper craftsmanship appealing and
    dangerous,

like an unknown religion full of Celtic rituals and engirdled with
    blood sacrifices.
The city ghosting from sight like the sleep's feisty door is darker
    now than before,

the fading light dancing slow like the floor of a funhouse that
    suddenly gives way.
Skin of animals, the vowels of reddish brick dust—surely there is
    only enough time

for one last messiah.  Ice, fire, whimper and bang, in the
    trumpeting sky of fire,
the tide gushes back in a glassy wash of fish, and the cosmos comes
    together,

its final headline: tender, frightening, the blossom of life bristles
    foolish, still red.

# WILLIAM BRONK'S PARADOXICAL
## ACCOMPLISHMENT

*Metaphor of Trees and Last Poems.* William Bronk. Jersey City: Talisman House Publishers, 1999.

*Henry Weinfield*

William Bronk died in February, 1999, shortly after his eighty-first birthday. He had been suffering from emphysema for many years, and for several had been attached to an oxygen line, but his poetic production had not flagged. Indeed, he often told friends in these last years that it was poetry that was keeping him alive. His most recent volume of poems, *All of What We Loved,* had appeared in 1998, and at his death, not only had he completed a new collection, *Metaphor of Trees,* but a number of poems in addition. This final, posthumous volume includes a poem that Bronk may have composed the day of his death and that was found beside his body. Like most of the poems he wrote during the last ten years, these are short (some only two or three lines long), aphoristic, declarative (sometimes to the point of being didactic), occasionally gnomic, and in the plain style that he had long cultivated. Bronk's muse spoke to him usually at night while he was asleep, and when he rose in the morning he would write that day's poem down. He revised more than he liked to admit, but very often the final version of a poem is exactly what he initially heard.

I rank Bronk as one of the two or three most important American poets of the post-war period. His roots are in Frost and Stevens (among earlier twentieth-century poets), and it was largely through Stevens that he developed the stylistic mastery that is already in evidence in *The World, The Worldless,* the great collection he published with New Directions in 1964. From Stevens, Bronk derived the loose iambic pentameter line that allowed him the spontaneity and flexibility to craft an original and philosophically radical vision into poems of great power. What Bronk took from Stevens was not the gaudiness of "Sea Surface Full of Clouds," say, but the plainness of "The Snow Man," but in Bronk's voice that plainness took on a prophetic cast that is not present in Stevens, and a grandeur that is perhaps more somber than what is heard in the earlier poet.

Bronk's greatest work, by and large, is to be found in *Life Supports: New and Collected Poems,* the volume he published in 1981 with North Point

Press (now sadly defunct), which won the American Book Award for 1982. (This volume has now been reissued by Talisman House, the publisher of Bronk's later years.) Bronk published ten subsequent collections including this one (not including the edition of *Selected Poems* that I edited for New Directions in 1995), and these contain many marvelous poems—poems of far greater value than what the inflated reputations of our time have produced—but on the whole, I think that there was a falling off. In the poetry of Bronk's greatest period, there is a balance (so rare in American poetry) between the prophetic visionary and the meticulous craftsman. The "redundancy quotient" was always rather high in Bronk's work because of the persistence with which he articulated an essentially unwavering vision, but the language was so vibrant in the poetry of the period of the sixties to the early eighties that somehow this didn't matter. In the later work it does matter because craft has been so thoroughly subsumed by vision that the boundaries between one poem and the next tend to disappear. And as Blake said, the greatness of any art depends on the clarity of the bounding line.

In the best of these late poems, there is a starkness and simplicity that reminds me as much of the pre-Socratic philosophers as of anything in the poetic tradition—but we forget that the pre-Socratics were, in fact, poets. Except for its ironic title, "Goes Way Back," for example, is pure Parmenides—if Parmenides had written in a twentieth-century American idiom:

> Whatever is is in the present tense.
> When it no longer is we see it was
> a misperception they had, not a thing
> that really is. Is always was. (17)

"It must be abstract," said Stevens, but a poem like this one cultivates a kind of abstraction—joined to a simplicity of phrasing—which is not exactly in fashion in contemporary American poetry. It is a lovely poem, if not quite a great one. What disturbs me (slightly) is not its slightness, but the way in which the poem wavers between free verse and metricality. The first two lines (with the delicate enjambment to the third) are iambic pentameter; the third seems to go fuzzy in the middle of the line, and the fourth is iambic tetrameter. One could easily "fix" the third and fourth lines to make them pentameter ("a misperception that they had and not / a thing that really is. Is always was"), but Bronk would undoubtedly have said that this isn't what he *heard,* and in any event he seems to follow Stevens in wavering between the freedom of Whitman and Williams and a more formal pentameter line, between the immediacy of voice and the impersonality of meter.

At their best, the very slightness of these poems gives them point and accentuates what one might call their play of *grammar*, the way in which the resources of language are played off against the conception. A three-line poem entitled "Eternity" (and how many poets today have the nerve to entitle poems "Eternity"?) can illustrate the point:

> Always isn't at any particular time
> so everness is also a neverness.
> At times, we are more comfortable with that.

This is the real "language poetry," it seems to me, because it assumes what poetry had always assumed in the past, but what it seems no longer to assume (and I include the so-called "Language Poets" in this): that the language of a poem can internally reflect the external conception, and that poetic *tension* inheres in this process of reflexivity. But the third line, which I think is only apparently flat, has something of a Robert-Frost-cracker-barrel-American-sage-aw-shucks quality; though certainly at a tonal remove from the tensile feeling of the first two lines, I think it somehow works.

The increasing abstractness of Bronk's style, it is now clear (he has a poem in *Life Supports* entitled "The Increasing Abstractness of Language" [179]), is the analogue for an Old Testament-cum-Calvinist vision in which all graven images are not only false but beside the point:

> The real name, should there be one,
> couldn't be spoken. The image given to man
> was unimagined, the image not to be graved.
> From the beginning, both god and man
> were set apart from everything spoken and seen
> and were only uncertainly sensed some by some. ("Storied," 23)

The irony here is that it is not only God that can't be imaged (or imagined) but man as well. ("Some by some" is a risk, but I think it pans out in the end.)

In their slightness, also, these poems accentuate the pathos of our relationship to the infinite:

> The marks we make to give us whens and wheres
> are inside other marks and they extend

to even larger ones until we find
the marks are marks but not on anything. ("Demarcation," 41)

This sort of pathos, which has always been the hallmark of Bronk's
work—and which connects him to a writer like Pascal—can extend from
the abstractness of cosmic space to the immediacy of human intimacy
and love:

The loved is not that person the lover loves
but what that person holds in the lover's sight
and holds sometimes not knowing what it holds
and could be anyone no matter who
because it's not that person that the lover loves.
("Du Côté de Chez Marcel," 48)

Always in Bronk there is a strange dialectic between the aesthetic formality of the poems and the sense of formlessness they describe, between the
epigrammatic concision and ironic wit of their style and the manner in
which their thought is aimed at totality or at the absolute:

In order for order we think invariant time,
invariant space and of all in earthly terms
as walls, say, ceilings and level floors,
as beginning somewhere, ending somewhere else.
But, even to say no walls, no floors, no ends,
even as negatives, these aren't the words
for an all that resists whatever order we make. ("Resistance," 100)

What do we make of a poetry which, while putting its faith in clarity
and simplicity, as far as its presentation is concerned, is so remorselessly
transcendental in its vision as to countenance no human (merely human)
touchstones or accomplishments? A three-line poem entitled "Fides et
Ratio," coming at the end of a volume which comes at the end of a long life
in poetry, raises this question:

The final accomplishment would be to know
the emptiness of any accomplishment
—to have that pleasure at the end of it.

Bronk's accomplishment (with its manifold pleasures) is now complete, and while his place in twentieth-century poetry is, I think, assured, we shall be interrogating the nature of that paradoxical accomplishment for many years to come.

# STREET-SMART SWAGGER & TENDRESSE

*Green Sees Things in Waves.* August Kleinzahler.
Farrar Straus Giroux, 1998.

*Andrew Osborn*

> Though a quarrel in the streets is a thing to
> be hated, the energies displayed in it are fine.
> —Keats

August Kleinzahler is a *flâneur* for our times, resolutely sniffing the city's corners for chance verse, demotic speech patterns, instances of authentic humanity. A son of North Jersey, he has written both sides of the George Washington Bridge, evinced the boarding-house and bar scenes of Montreal and Vancouver, stalked Jean Follain through Paris, and, in San Francisco, taken the Haight, Golden Gate Park, and Chinatown into his bootsoles. "*Another side / of the city* [...] *uno altro aspetto*," he explains to a Signora "in an alley below Mission, smelling / something much too intimate." Everywhere he goes, he achieves such street-level intimacy. As suggested by the titles of his first three collections—*Storm Over Hackensack, Earthquake Weather,* and *Red Sauce, Whiskey and Snow*—Kleinzahler also consistently attends to climate and its swing-partner, mood. I was therefore not surprised to find in his latest book, *Green Sees Things in Waves,* a piece titled "Snow in North Jersey." Nor was I surprised that its narrating presence, initially observing from some remove on-high, gets drawn down to take on the vernacular of its blue-collar subjects:

> while in the upstairs of a thousand duplexes
> with the TV on, cancers tick    tick    tick
> and the snow continues to fall and blanket
> these crowded rows of frame and brick
> with their heartbreaking porches and castellations
> and the red '68 Impala on blocks
> and Joe he's drinking again and Myra's boy Tommy
> in the old days it would have been a disgrace
> and Father Keenan's not been having a good winter[.]

Later we hear *'ho dear* and "lordjesussaveus they're still making babies." Such plights and gripes are the one-off flakes of this snowfall.

There's something here also of the undiscriminating snow in Joyce's "The Dead," which, falling general all over Ireland, levels differences in social status as it mutes the landscape's contours. But Kleinzahler is not interested in allusion for its own sake (the title "On First Looking into Joseph Cornell's Diaries" being an exception) so much as in adapting what has been shown to work for new purposes. Moving on from the railyards and bus barns, his state-side flurries fall no less on the "big houses along the river bluff," but there the snippets of speech cease and the owners are called "swells"—as if empathic access were cut off with the weather-proofing. The poem's class-consciousness heightens and is formalized at the end.

> It's snowing on us all
> and on a three-story *fix-up* off of Van Vorst Park
> a young lawyer couple from Manhattan bought
> where for no special reason in back of a closet
> a thick, dusty volume from the '30s sits open
> with a broken spine and smelling of mildew
> to a chapter titled *Social Realism*

Presumably the lawyer couple will eventually fix up their *fix-up*, and out will go the broken-spined reminder of all that the first five-sixths of the poem showed was worthy of attention. Kleinzahler fixes it there instead, against the amnesia of upward mobility.

Elsewhere he is similarly ill-at-ease, or maybe just watchful, about what happens when one shapes life with all its jagged edginess into an aesthetic object. It can be a lot like gentrification. That's not always a bad thing, but it's important to keep an eye on what's getting gutted or spackled over. When "Whole floors, / [are] broken up and carted off" in "Where Galluccio Lived" (*Earthquake*), there's a well-timed pause, then the lyric speaker reflects: "Memory stinks, like good marinara sauce. / You never get that garlic smell / out of the walls." The point being, I suppose, that whether memory stinks good or stinks bad, sometimes it's worth catching a whiff of, remembering. Poets who routinely opt for open, indeterminate structures or put a fine finish on everything thereby forfeit much of their chosen art's mnemonic advantage. In *Green*, "The Conversation" shifts the focus of such concerns from urban renewal to interpersonal relationships.

> This then was the conversation
> [...]
> That drove all ahead of it
> A great wave or wind
> That tore apart the very ground
> That sent up a wall of debris
> That would leave nothing

if, as Kleinzahler posits, one

> Put one's own arm
> One's hand
> Down into the engine of its force
> To know its workings[.]

By the end of this narrow, sparsely punctuated poem, having likened the conversation again to a whirlwind and upped the ante ("Why not") with a "biblical reek," he has nevertheless seen it scaled down into something "kept in the vestibule / An ornament / A kinetic sculpture / In the corner / On a stand / An *objet d'art*." Who has not had such a conversation? It seethes, a malignant presence, and yet too worked-at to part with or forget. Uncharacteristically, Kleinzahler offers not so much as a syllable of the conversation itself; instead, the relentless morphing involved in his attempts to contain it convey its menace.

Kleinzahler aims at keeping such tensions keen. Albeit somewhat up-the-establishment in demeanor, he is too wily a craftsman to go unheeded by academe. Alloyed of his own brand of social realism and eclectic scholarship, then refined with an ear tuned by Basil Bunting and Thelonious Monk, his poems help readers of all walks appreciate the rich store of rhythms, images, and emotions among the down-and-out without feeling patronized or preached to. The book's title poem exemplifies his talky affability. In the space of twenty or so breath-long lines the eponymous "Green"—whom I had taken to be a color with some abstract agency like that of Wallace Stevens' Phosphor "Reading by His Own Light"—has become "our boy," though we've since learned that he suffers from perceptual lag and hallucinated intimidation and will learn that these maladies result from an LSD overdose back when. If, thinking back to Joyce, the message Gabriel reads in the snow is *for all your learned opinions and eloquence, you are no more elect or alive than* . . ., Kleinzahler's cautionary message is more invitational: don't let creature comforts deprive you of the troves an eye and ear to the underside affords. Don't let your schooling narrow your bandwidth. Take time to smell the garlic.

Unlike Whitman, Kleinzahler is one of the roughs by his own choosing. This has been evident from the start but is foregrounded in new work like "What the Science of the Ancients Told," a sinuous long poem about the pulse diagnostics ("Sphygmology") practiced in medieval Cathay and by the 10th-century Arab physician-philosopher Avicenna. This poet indulgently flaunts a love of esoteric, often tongue-torquing words and phrases. "52 Pick-Up" (the title acknowledges the poem's let-the-cards-fall-where-they-may lack of ambition) consists solely of a dual-column list of 52 samples: "Suzerainty," Noam Chomsky's "Colorless green ideas sleep furiously," "Huitzilopochtli," "Sforzato," "Korsakoff's Syndrome," "Guelph." When such roughage crops up in the course of a more narrative poem, you can tell the poet's feelin' his oats, and Kleinzahler feels his oats regularly. Thus, we get poems like "Glossalalia All the Way to Buffalo," featuring Colonel Vladimir Khotchokakov (schoolbus humor). But he restrains himself admirably when the mood or tone requires, stripping down his diction as for the black-and-white and eventually pictographic-seeming scene of "Silver Gelatin." From a high-rise window, a domestic is (optically) "caught through a net of griseous branches":

> She leans forward now, pushing in haste.
> At her own now extreme angle
>
> and with the black coat and hat,
> the pram underneath her,
> the snow underfoot,
> she looks, for all the world, from here,
>
> a broken-off piece of Chinese ideogram
> moving across the page.

I love the austere delicacy of this poem. It is Pound's "In a Station of the Metro" writ larger. Kleinzahler's one lexical luxury, "griseous" in lieu of "grey," is warranted, imbuing the scene with a granularity. With the same efficiency the lack of a *like* in that final would-be simile bespeaks the broken-off-ness.

One sign of Kleinzahler's remarkable versatility is that despite his intense commitment to the urban preterite, he has a real knack for waxing urbane. For lyrics commemorating courtships of the not so distant past (his own), he will sometimes don the rhetorical flourish of courtly rhythms, diction, and syntax. In the second section of the charming "They Ofttimes Choose," his Corinnas, Megs, and Philomels, well-pleased,

> Then take their leave but are not truly gone,
> for amidst the cushions and disarray
> bracelets and earrings, a kerchief I'll find.
>
> They, who are not careless in other ways,
> are careless neither in what they leave behind
> [...]
> How well these ladies do contrive, how well,
> to keep me in thrall with their sweet neglect.

Equal parts Wyatt and Herrick. You can almost hear the harpsichord plink-plinking in the background.

Of a piece, albeit less mannered, are the last five lines of "Watching Young Couples with an Old Girlfriend on Sunday Morning." Having made mention of MTV, tattoo ubiquity, and huevos rancheros, each anti-aesthetic and somewhat alienating, he asks, "Or do I recoil from their youthfulness and health?"

> Oh, not recoil, just fail to see ourselves.
> And yet, this tenderness between us that remains
>
> was mortared first with a darkness that got loose, a frenzy,
> we still, we still refuse to name.

Note how the same consonants recur, not to rhyme but to swarm, at the ends of those final lines: *remains* (/r/-/m/-/n/-/z/), *frenzy* (/f/-/r/-/n/-/z/), *refuse to name* (/r/-/f/-/z/ /n/-/m/). That's the kind of phonetic finesse almost anyone will appreciate on some level—probably unconsciously, grinning all the while—but too few poets aim for these days. The anti-eloquence set veer away with a theory-bound vengeance, while the New Formalists, who ostensibly strive for such effects, cheat themselves with rigidity. The same thing goes for metrics. Having laid down a perfect iambic pentameter line ("Oh, not recoil . . ."), Kleinzahler relies on his departure therefrom to register the pacing, the give-and-take, of cognitive pursuit and repression. Were "a frenzy" not held overtime in the penultimate line, the stymied caesura between "we still" and "we still" would dissolve; "a frenzy" would seem a glib denomination of that darkness, and the poem would end in oxymoron, the unnamed named.

Despite Kleinzahler's ranging, an elsewhere uncommon combination of brutish virility and empathic vulnerability ("tenderness . . . mortared first with a darkness") pervades. It was at the heart of "The Sausage-Master of Minsk" (*Storm*), whose hardy, pungent hero pursues a "half-formed" girl and ends up with mussed hair "interlaced with fine, pubescent yarn." One could hear it in that same early volume's "Vikings of the Air," whose speaker puts on a piratical swagger to bark orders—"*Dump the goods, you scallywags, save this balloon*"—but is inwardly an even-tempered optimist, reflecting, "Happily, [...] we can buy air by dropping what we must." *Red Sauce*'s epigraph, from "Louisiana blues man" Herman E. Johnson, speaks to the same mix: "*So my life was just that way, to keep out of trouble, / drink my little whisky, an' go an' do little ugly things / like that, but in a cue-tee way.*" Finally, in *Green*, it is the conversant canine of "The Dog Stoltz," so modest in its fiction, that most poignantly perpetuates this signature motif. Kleinzahler demonstrates devotion more readily for animals than humans and when attending to humans is most alert to their animal instincts and needs. Stoltz, "part bull and something else," is something else indeed; he not only talks, he is planning an essay on the war poet Sassoon. Kleinzahler's human persona, the "I" of this poem, eulogizes the mongrel as "first beast, then scholar, then abject and adored." When he then asks parenthetically, "Say, who among us does not care to be undressed?" he is, I think, acknowledging, in the devious, sideways-glancing way of dreams, that Stoltz is a second version of himself in doggy dishabille. Allowing for some hyperbole, the brief pedigree suits Kleinzahler's poetic persona to a T, and could have served me as the title of this review. What's interesting, then, is the rhetorical, human dream-self's disowning of the seemingly more-at-home-with-himself animal scholar. He protests too much (twice) that Stoltz does not belong to him and significantly slips into the present tense even as he avows an over-and-done-with separation:

> He was not my dog, you know. He simply followed me out
> of what can only have been a very fine home,
> such were his graces, his recondite tastes.
> But he was a killer, too, and rather smelled.
> I cannot accommodate another animal now, please understand.
> I am between places. I will yearn for Stoltz, but no.

I don't think Kleinzahler could abandon the dog Stoltz in him even if he truly wished to. I for one do not wish him to, for the pure products of Kleinzahler's own grace and recondite tastes, killer (prosodic) instinct, street-smart swagger, and *tendresse* are winning. *Green Sees Things in Waves* deserves readers in droves.

# PRYNNE'S *POEMS*

*Poems.* J.H. Prynne. Newcastle upon Tyne, UK: Bloodaxe Books, 1999.

*Devin Johnston*

When a prominent writer associated with Language poetry visited
Chicago to give a reading last year, a student asked her what contemporary
poet she reads with the greatest enthusiasm. She answered—without
elaborating— "Jeremy Prynne." And though Prynne's readership in the
United States has been minuscule, it has included a devoted following
among experimental poets. Perhaps ironically, such poets often wield
considerable influence regarding what gets taught, written about, and
sometimes even read. Until now, the fugitive nature of Prynne's publications, as well as his reticence to give readings or engage in self-promotion,
have not permitted a wider readership (though such qualities have contrib-
uted to his mystique among the devoted). With the publication of this
volume of collected poems, from a major British press, that situation may
change. Recent issues of *The New Yorker* have included a reader's poll for the
best volume of poetry of 1999: Prynne's book was listed along with those of
Louise Glück, David Ferry, John Koethe, and Sherod Santos. Though *The
New Yorker* has little clout among readers of poetry these days, such a
grouping must come as a surprise to those who have sought out Prynne's
pamphlets through obscure channels over the past decades.

Unsurprisingly, the vagaries in Prynne's reputation have little bearing
on the actual poetry—indeed, I often find the discussion surrounding
Prynne at odds with the experience of reading his poems. Prynne was a
friend of the American poet Charles Olson, and has written critical essays
on *The Maximus Poems*: in attempting to locate Prynne's difficult and
original writing in a tradition, readers and critics have often lumped him in
a post-modern, post-Olson, and essentially American lineage. Such a direct
influence from Olson does exist in contemporary British poetry—one
might think of Allen Fisher's long poem entitled *Place*, which transposes the
Olsonian *omphalos* from Gloucester, Massachusetts, to South London.
Prynne, on the other hand, writes in an abstracted lyrical mode, a surprisingly urbane and elegant discourse that bears little similarity to Olson's flat,
rangy lines. Prynne suppressed his first volume of poetry, *Force of Circumstance and Other Poems* (1962), from this collected volume. In these early

poems, such as "Mining for Flint," one can detect the centrally British derivation of his style:

> Below this fronded heath the casualness
> Is closer packed and waiting for the blow
> From the moon's incisive stare. Down to the black
> Siliceous lode this glacial calm makes slow
> Deliberate descent; the night's attack
> Upon the branching daylight's understress.[1]

Such desolated landscapes, invoked with a cool eye for metallurgical or geological detail, are strongly reminiscent of those one finds in W.H. Auden's early "Who stands, the crux left of the watershed," and in some of Thomas Hardy's poems as well. Intermittently throughout his career, this landscape returns as the ground for Prynne's political concerns. In the *Oval Window* (1983), the rural landscape takes on considerable ambivalence and complexity:

> Now the willows on the river are hazy like mist
> and the end is hazy like the meaning
> which bridges its frozen banks. In the field
> of view a prismatic blur adds on
> rainbow skirts to the outer leaves.
> They appropriated not the primary
> conditions of labour but their results;
> the waters of spring cross under
> the bridge, willow branches dip.
> The denial of Feudalism in China
> always leads to political errors, of an
> essentially Trotskyist order:
> Calm is all nature as a resting wheel.
> The red candle flame shakes.  (337)

In such cases, Prynne's fluid movement between a geographical scene, a phenomenology of seeing, and the political implications of both (in both metaphorical and literal terms) would seem to be central to his point. In the modern world, he suggests, even the most pastoral scene undergoes a "cognitive mapping" onto a global or abstract space.

Many of Prynne's most compelling poems investigate such concerns through an overt lyricism—a condensed yet peculiarly spacious mode that leads one to consider its place in a lyrical tradition. Take, for example, a short poem from *The White Stones* (1969) entitled "Love"—which I find to be one of his most appealing:

> Noble in the sound which
> marks the pale ease
> of their dreams, they ride
> the bel canto of our
> time: the patient en-
> circlement of Narcissus &
> as he pines I too
> am wan with fever,
> have fears which set
> the vanished child above
> reproach. Cry as you
> will, take what you
> need, the night is young
> and limitless our greed. (118)

Though the "pale ease / of their dreams" is a touch sardonic in its Keatsian rhetoric, the poem seems genuinely concerned with desire. If desire locates the lyric self, Prynne suggests, limitless desire (or greed) renders that self unbound. In the lyric tradition, one often encounters a desire so strong it seems to broach the boundaries of the self. In Prynne's verse, the boundaries between erotic and economic forms of desire also dissolve. As he concludes in *Kitchen Poems* (1968), an exploration of desire often charts the disappearance of the self: "we give the name of / our selves to our needs. / We want what we are" (20).

Much of Prynne's poetry could be characterized as tracking the capricious movement of thought or consciousness, though it is not entirely clear that such cognitions are embodied in any sense. In this respect, Prynne's poetry has a general resemblance to that of Ashbery or—closer to home— Tom Raworth. Raworth and Prynne, along with a few others, have been dubbed "the Cambridge School" (mostly because they both live there). In temperament, the two poets are quite distinct: Raworth is sharp and funny, and comes closer to Ashbery's ability to encompass the highs and lows of culture in a single bound; Prynne, on the other hand, tends to be more circumscribed and elevated in tone. Yet they share a poetic technique for which they could take out a patent. Both poets often use line-breaks to slip into another frame of reference, enjambing one thought into another without any disruption of syntax. The resulting lines tend to move faster than our ability to process. Such is the case in a poem from *White Stones* (1969) entitled "Foot and Mouth":

> Every little shift towards comfort is a manoeuvre
> of capital loaned off into the jungle of interest: see
> how the banks celebrate their private season, with
> brilliant swaps across the Atlantic trapeze. Such del-
> icate abandon: we hold ourselves comfortingly braced
> beneath, a safety-net of several millions & in what
> we shall here call north Essex the trend is certainly
> towards ease, time off to review those delicious values
> traced in frost on the window or which wage-labour
> used to force to the Friday market. Actually as I look
> out the silly snow is collapsing into its dirty self
> again... (107)

Each line snaps back into the next, and it is only through reflection that the seemingly disparate elements begin to cohere. In this case, the experience of reading the poem is instructive, for it is collapsing two spheres we tend to hold apart—the transcendental world of high finance and personal experience.

At times, over the course of this career-spanning volume, the obscurity of Prynne's verse proves frustrating—particularly given its insistent gestures toward ideation. His strong rhetoric occasionally verges on mannered or pedantic, with the lingering insistence that the experience of the poem is that of the postmodern condition. This frustration can derive from Prynne's arch formality as well, which is rarely concerned with "musicality," but rather with a vaguely ironized patterning of thought. Such is the case, I think, in the following poem from *Into the Day* (1972):

> What swims in the eye
> is mortal dread, solar
> flare. The ear spins
> with sharp cries, there
> is shear at the flowline.
> Honour thy father,
> anguish as the sign

deflects through water,
into port. The shell
crossing is sport,
they are childlike
and their limbs intact. (214)

The half-emerging scene—involving an Oedipal relationship? and a sea-side locale?—is in itself compelling. Yet the irregular but full rhymes here suggest an irony that is difficult to account for in the poem's content. The result is an invocation of lyric affect and its simultaneous dismissal, which can seem a little coy. At such moments, Prynne recalls the involution—and resulting frustrations—of Louis Zukofsky at his most hermetic.

Over the last few decades, the mannered quality in Prynne's poetry has been filtered out to some degree, and he has favored a slighter, more obscure, but more lively mode, usually consisting of a sequence of short lyrics. In *Word Order* (1989), for instance, one finds,

We were bribed and bridled
with all we had, in
the forms of marriage
close to the target, very near
we held out brightly

that, there is a door shut
in whispered turbulence of the air
flow, echo virus inversion
in cardiac shadow to see over
the lights of common day. (362)

Though not much subject to paraphrase, one detects in the diction Prynne's characteristic concerns—an erotic relationship, thermodynamics, private and public forms of identity. Indeed, such poems may rely on some familiarity with Prynne's earlier work in order to identify the key elements at play. In its abstract lyricism, this recent mode may be comparable to that of any number of experimental poets now writing in Britain and America. Yet its elegance is a rare accomplishment: one senses an economy at work before the utility of that economy becomes apparent (if it ever does). It may be this quality—a floating sense of urgency—that has gained the trust of a growing number of readers.

Prynne is already the subject of one collection of essays—*Nearly Too Much: The Poetry of J.H. Prynne*, edited by N.H. Reeve and Richard Kettridge—as well as numerous essays published in small poetry journals. It is worth noting that this process of exegesis and evaluation already exceeds the criticism on many more "prominent" poets, and I suspect that it will only increase in coming years. Prynne's commentators tend to value his work for its excess of signification and resistance to authoritative interpretation. Such reasoning tends to place an ethical value on difficulty and uncertainty because such qualities instill vigilance and hard work in readers and critics. Though I sometimes find poetry shallow or trivial, I never find it "too easy"—and I thus remain skeptical of such reasoning. It may be that we link reading poetry to the critical enterprise too closely these days. Whatever impossible hermeneutic challenges Prynne's poetry poses to the critic, it offers many mysterious pleasures to the reader. Uncertainty—of the sort one encounters in Prynne's verse—often sends commentators irritably reaching after fact and reason, while readers are happy to linger in that state. Beyond partisan debates over his place in contemporary poetry, Prynne has developed a deeply original body of writing, and this collection offers rewards commensurate with its demands.

---

[1] J. H. Prynne, *Force of Circumstance and Other Poems* (London: Routledge and Kegan Paul, 1962), 25.

# TWO USES OF MIND: OR THE ART OF ABSENCE

*Atchley* by David Green. Station Hill Press, 1998. 120pp. Pb. $12.95.

The illustration on the front cover of this dense little book is very appropriate. It is a painting by Magritte, "La Reproduction Interdite." We view the back of a man viewing himself, the back of himself, in a mirror. Self deflection rather than self reflection? A hoax? A serious spoof? A memoir? Fiction? A "fiction"? The "truths" of the author's life disguised and embellished in order to convey Truths—autobiography as biography (pace Gertrude Stein/Alice B)? The impedimenta of the first section contain false references embedded in sometimes very long footnotes (pace Lawrence Stern). Even the acknowledgments are suspect; he thanks the HRHRC at Austin, Texas "for their helpfulness in providing access to...Atchley's letters and manuscripts in their possession." One wonders if perhaps some library intern, after reading this, is working overtime to try and find the materials which now seem mysteriously absent.

But what is this book about? We ask the old banal question. It is about itself, as the young Beckett said of Joyce's early *Work in Progress* which was to become *FW*. But a work of art is never entirely about itself despite our modernist/post-modernist forebears.

It is about its perceivers, its readers. As in *Rezeptionsesthetik*. About its writerly readers, ideally, in the Barthesean (*S/Z*) sense. But this opens a can of worms, questions about the inviolable integrity of the work of art, and by extension the whole problem of the decline of our culture due to making "art" cater to the banalities of non-artist perceivers. And a work of art is about—of course—other art. This book in particular triggers this reader to images, associations, to see/hear paraphrases, ideas or even some quoshed quotatoes from other characters, other authors, other texts. *Atchley* the book and Atchley the character are about...well, let Atchley speak:

> "My work has grown stale to me. The greatest gift is to be able to re-create the world through one's words, to appreciate its colors, dark and bright. And yet I take the colors and make them dull, digging into the ground beneath the gardens...to find what soil and rock supports the color, ...as if the cold dark earth could explain the iridescence of the iris. Why do I make this effort to explore another's world and not my own, to establish my presence as the elaboration of another's?" (36)

Yes, we murder to dissect. This, after he has written a letter to say that he has met "this fellow Green at Birkbeck" and "didn't quite know what to make of him." (Suddenly one thinks of *At Swim-Two-Birds*, whose fictional characters comment on and annoy their author, himself a fictional character created by the book's pseudonymous author, Flann O'Brien)

At times, *Atchley* seems to be about challenging futility—the Futility described to me once as Wonder by a psychiatrist—that we can never analyze or dissect to find the causes of beauty; the integrity of essential reality is not divisible. Nor explainable. Nor should we wish it so, he believed, this sensitive psychiatrist.

But *Atchley* can't leave well enough alone. The book (for want of a better name) wants to question assumptions down to the bone: "...author and character are nothing more than events in the mind of the reader; in fact how they exist in the mind of the reader is more important to who they are than who they really are....It is always possible that some unscrupulous scholar has created a writer by the name of Atchley to question the assumptions and strategies of critical theory." (11-12)

Perhaps the author is a phenomenon of the text [but then who created the text?]. Green observes: "Atchley is really saying two things...that the person who does the writing is not a single unified entity, but is rather the provisional amalgam of a changing environment, literary influences, impulses, skills, and so on; and second, that this person only becomes an author by virtue of the text...as understood by those who engage in [it]." (14-15)

Do such questions and concerns hold up over time, or are they merely fashionable, trendy concerns of our post-modern times?

To return to the quote from page 36: One thinks of Sartre's Roquentin's final resolution in *Nausea.* To give up devoting his life to writing about the life of another (a DWM, actually) and to write a new kind of book, one that would make its readers ashamed of their Existence. Is Atchley ashamed of his existence? Or is he annoyed that he hasn't got more of it? The presence of absence or the absence of presence...?

"He doubts whether it is possible to eliminate the authorial influence from a work altogether." Well, who cares? After the death of God, must we kill off authors now? Pride and self immolation—if the author can eliminate his Traces from his own work, then...? The autonomous text, devoid of Voice? And what about James Joyce's authorial intrusions in *Dubliners,* how his Narrative Voice mimics the voice and language of a character so that we are taken in, as by Maria in "Clay," and then subtly given distance by a single word, such as "ferreted"? Is this not akin to Romantic Irony? Is there not a tradition from which contemporary authors such as Green or Atchley still draw, one that at least debunks the most artificial device of all, the omniscient narrator?

When we look more closely at that Magritte painting we notice a blue book on the mantel, part of its cover reflected in the mirror; but while the back of the man appears in the reflection rather than his front, the reflection of the book is as normal, with the lines of letters on its surface mirrored as in life. So, are we to infer something that at least the book designer, Susan Quasha, saw—that while the man/author/mind is hiding the self, the text is to be read as "normal"?

Not only has the author, Green, doubled himself in Atchley (his mother's maiden name, incidentally)—sometimes the narrative is in the first person, sometimes in the third person. The book itself falls into two: a meditation on writing, "The Art of Absence, a pickayune questioning process" and, *Landfall,* a picaresque questing tale filled with glorious sensory description, flora and fauna of Gallicia, and the teller's physical creaturehood in the existential, historical, phenomenal world. Something for the mind, something for the body. A tour de force of collaboration or symbiosis between the left brain and the right brain of one skull collaborating, or at least contained in, one text.

But then, I recall an old e-mail from Green who protests, "Since I was trying to avoid writing about anything in particular, I used description to fill the void, to create wonder rather than thought." At the quest's inevitable and ideal end, we are treated to a self reflexive pun, the "deep green" surface of the sea. And other words give us other companions: "buoyant stern" and "lilac flakes of light" and "small sargasso"—do we not think of Eliot, of Pound, of the pre-Raphaelites, of Saint Brendan?

He does not say so, but Green's Atchley's boat "responded gaily." For me. Like *FW,* this book wants a return to the sea. A Vichian *ricorso.*

Well, Green is deep, or at least "his" Atchley is striving for both depth and simplicity. The mind's attempts at self perception are valiant and perhaps ever inconclusive. The nature of an artistic text is never reducible to a definitive explanation or theory, nor is the beautiful, nor is the sublime. It has taken me nine months to read this book (with maps.) I don't mind. I suggest you do the same.

—*Alison Armstrong*

## EDITORS SELECT

Corinne Demas, *Eleven Stories High: Growing Up in Stuyvesant Town*, 1948-1968, SUNY Press, 2000. *NDR* contributor Demas' childhood memoir is a remarkable portrait of a vanished world, but not a vanished place. The social history it captures is important, presenting the story of a transitional generation of women, suspended between the quietism of the American Dream of the post-war era of the 1950s and the tumultuous upheavals to come at the end of the 1960s. A vivid and paradoxical picture of both urban America and domestic life once lived, captured by a writer of lyric strengths and fastidious intellect.

Craig Nova, *Brook Trout and the Writing Life*, The Lyons Press, 1999. Acclaimed novelist Nova's first book of nonfiction, a brief, but lapidary look at life from a trout fisher's oblique eye view. Though reminiscent of Hemingway (if "Papa" had been a dedicated family man), Nova limns a life suspended both from and in time. A new age *The Compleat Angler*, the reading of which Edward Dahlberg (who Nova admiringly quotes—unacknowledged) once long ago remarked, would make anyone "more quiet."

Peter Ho Davis, *Equal Love*, Houghton Mifflin Co., 2000. Ho's second collection (after *The Ugliest House in the World*, 1997) and equally remarkable. Ho is a transnational, a citizen of the world, and his stories' range is far-reaching. San Francisco's Chinatown, rustic Britain, and rural New Hampshire, Ho takes up residence in any or all of these milieus and calls it home. Ho is one of the best of the younger generation of short story writers.

Michael Martone, *The Flatness and Other Landscapes*, The University of Georgia Press, 2000. *NDR* contributor Martone's new collection of essays won the 1998 Associated Writing Programs Award for Creative Nonfiction. He is one of the best illuminators of the midwestern triptych, its people, places and propensities, and throughout these various entertaining and insightful essays, his thoroughly geodesic eye surveys the horizontal imperatives of the most interior of our nation's states.

Jaimy Gordon, *Bogeywoman*, Sun & Moon Classics, 1999. Readers of Gordon's *Shamp of the City-Solo* (1980) and *She Drove Without Stopping* (1990) will not be disappointed with *Bogeywoman*. In a breathtaking tour de force Gordon's narrator, the Bogeywoman of the title, takes the dazzled reader along for 350 pages of riffs and rants as fully energized as a Charlie Parker solo. In the psychiatric ward of a hospital, she becomes a member of a musical group called the Bug Motels and meets the amazing Madame Zuk—a psychiatrist, and much more than that as well. A book for readers who still love language and who like their language charged. The best nuthouse novel since *One Flew Over the Cuckoo's Nest.*

Joshua Barkan, *Before Hiroshima and Other Stories,* tobypress.com, 2000. Joshua Barkan's first volume of stories is one of the first titles to be published by The Toby Press, titles available only through their web site. The first story—a novella, really—is told by a Japanese intelligence officer who has discovered the importance of "The Pumpkin Project"—dummy bombs dropped at various locations around Japan to see if planes could carry heavy payloads like the "Fat Man" finally dropped on Hiroshima. The book is an impressive debut and the title story has been praised by Saul Bellow, among others. The other Toby Press titles are worth looking into as well. This program may represent one future, if not necessarily *the* future, of literary publishing.

Basil Bunting, *Complete Poems,* Bloodaxe, 2000. Bunting's many readers in this country will be delighted to discover that his work is back in print and available through the American distributor of Bloodaxe Books, Dufour Editions. Bunting's small but marvelous body of work is increasingly seen as among the major contributions to modernist writing. All of the familiar "Sonatas" are included—"Briggflatts," "The Spoils," "Villon"—along with the

odes, the translations, and a range of previously uncollected poems and versions (or "overdrafts," as he called them) from various poetries that engaged Bunting during his long life. The volume comes with a double cassette tape on which Bunting reads most of his major poems. He was one of the great performers of poetry. Hearing him read his own work is an enormous pleasure.

Michael S. Harper and Anthony Walton, editors, *The Vintage Book of African American Poetry,* Vintage, 2000. Harper and Walton have edited what may well become a definitve anthology. Beginning with poets like Phillis Wheatley, George Moses Horton, Frances E.W. Harper, and Paul Laurence Dunbar, the book represents familiar figures from the Harlem Renaissance and major writers such as Jean Toomer, Sterling A. Brown, Langston Hughes, Countee Cullen and Robert Hayden. The final third of the book turns to contemporary poets without lowering poetic standards (there's no hip hop; there's no rap). Selections from Gwendolyn Brooks, Derek Walcott, Etheridge Knight, Amiri Baraka, Lucille Clifton, Jay Wright, Rita Dove, Yusef Komunyakaa, and Michael Harper himself are substantial and original. The book includes only 50 poets from the colonial period to the present. It dares to exercise that rare thing these days—true editorial judgment.

William Borden, *Eurydice's Song*, St. Andrews College Press, 1999. Monotypes by Douglas Kinsey. Borden and Kinsey have produced a beautiful book on the theme of Orpheus and Eurydice. Readers of *Notre Dame Review* will be familiar with Kinsey's work. The rich full-page and double-page illustrations capture the eye as Borden's reinvention of the familiar myth captures the ear and mind. The originality of the poem is that it is told entirely from Eurydice's point of view. As Bordon says in a note, "I wondered if Orpheus, the rock star of ancient Greece, would have been all that attentive a husband, and if Eurydice might have been seduced into the underworld. Love, even true, passionate, knocked-out love, embraces ambivalence, uncertainty, and the improbability of having everything we desire."

Michael J. Rosen, editor, *Mirth of a Nation: The Best Contemporary Humor*, HarperCollins, 2000. An idea whose time has come, once again. Even the title is funny, as is the cover copy— "140 shots from the loose canon of American humor." The usual celebrity posse is here, along with some lesser-known humorists. Not quite the Algonquin Round Table, but a new millennium crew who create American humor of the sort that will not be found on the Fox Network.

David Huddle, *The Story of a Million Years*, Houghton Mifflin, 1999. Huddle, a master of the contemporary short story, has lashed a number of them together to create his first novel. He follows the example of many other novelists, whose own literary evolution let their first novels be linked short stories, with repeating characters, though Huddle has taken his time before making his triumphal debut. His novel is an elaborate minuet of secrets and relationships, following two couples and their interlacing lives. The first chapter was originally an award winning story, "Past My Future," the tale of a young teenager's affair with an older friend of the family. Done in the young women's voice, it shows Huddle's deepening craft and his exquisite control of the unexpected and the disturbing. One of the best first novels of 1999.

# CONTRIBUTORS

**Alison Armstrong** is the author of *The Joyce of Cooking* (Station Hill Press) and *"The Herne's Egg" by W.B. Yeats: The Manuscript Materials* (Cornell Unviersity Press). Her essays, short stories, poetry and reviews have appeared in diverse publications. She was a Founding Editor of *A James Joyce Broadsheet*, (U.K.), Fiction Editor at the *Kenyon Review* and a Contributing Editor to *Irish Literary Supplement*. She now lives in Greenwich Village. **Mike Barrett**, a poet, teaches at Moberly Area Community College in Missouri. **Jill Peláez Baumgaertner** is Professor of English at Wheaton College. Her collections of poetry include *Leaving Eden* (White Eagle Coffee Store), *Namings* (Franciscan University) and the forthcoming *Uprooted* (Chimney Hill). **Ace Boggess** of Huntington, West Virginia, has poems in *Concho River Review, Baltimore Review, Chaminade Literary Review,* and other journals. **Peg Boyers** is Executive Editor of *Salmagundi*. Poems from a book length series in the voice of Natalia Ginzburg have apppeared in *Paris Review, Partisan Review, Southern Review, New England Review, The New Criterion* and other magazines. **Jarda Cervenka** was born in Prague. He immigrated to Minnesota three decades ago and has traveled and lived on three continents. His collection of stories *Mal d' Afrique* won the Minnesota Voices contest and the collection *Revenge of Underwater Man* won the Richard Sullivan Prize for 2000 (Notre Dame Press). His story "Salima" was a runner up in the *Boston Review's* international fiction contest. **Nancy Donegan** is a lecturer in English at Brown University. She has published one book of poetry, *The Forked Rivers*, with Alice James Press. Her poems have appeared in *Tendril, Soundings/East, Writ* and *Willow Springs.* **Andrew Epstein's** poems and essays have appeared in such journals as *Verse, Raritan, Lungfull!, Ribot,* and *Combo.* He is finishing his Ph.D. in English at Columbia University, where he has been teaching for several years, and is working on a study of individualism and friendship in twentieth-century American poetry. **Reginald Gibbons'** most recent book of poems is *Homage to Longshot O'Leary* (Holy Cow! Press, 1999). A paperback edition of his novel *Sweetbitter* was issued in 1996 by Penguin, and his translation of Euripides' *Bacchae* will be published by Oxford University Press. From 1981 to 1997 he was the editor of *TriQuarterly* magazine, at Northwestern University, where he is currently a professor of English. **David Green**, a graduate of Notre Dame, has taught at universities in Spain, China, and the United States. He currently teaches at Boston University and is the author of the novel *Atchley.* **Robert Hahn** is the author of *No Messages*, his second major collection of poetry (following *All Clear*, University of South Carolina, 1996), which is the 2000 winner of the Ernest Sandeen Award and will be published by University of Notre Dame Press in the fall. Other poems by Hahn have appeared recently or will appear in *Paris Review, Yale Review, Partisan Review, Southwest Review*, and *Shenandoah*. **Glenna Holloway** is a native Tennessean who now lives in Naperville, Illinois. She is a silversmith, lapidary and enamelist. Her poetry has appeared in *Western Humanities Review, Michigan Quarterly Review, Spoon River Poetry Review, America* and many anthologies. **Devin Johnston** serves as poetry editor for *Chicago Review*, and has critical essays forthcoming in *Contemporary Literature* and *Callaloo*. His poems have appeared in *Fence, New American Writing, The Germ*, and elsewhere; his first volume of poems, *Telepathy*, is forthcoming from Paper Bark Press. **Eduardo Kac's** art is exhibited internationally and is in the permanent collections of the Museum of Modern Art in New York, Joan Flasch Artists' Book Collection, Chicago, and the Museum of Modern Art in Rio de Janeiro, Brazil, among others. In 1999 he was awarded the ICC Biennale Award (Tokyo). **R.M. Kinder** is author of *Sweet Angel Band*, a short-fiction collection published by Helicon Nine. Her most recent work appears or will appear in *Literal Latte, Other Voices, Southern Humanities Review, Descant* (Ontario), *Connecticut Review* and elsewhere. She is executive editor of *Pleiades* at Central Missouri State University, where she also coordinates the creative writing program. **Marilyn Krysl's** latest book is *How to Accommodate Men*, Coffee House, 1998. **Susan Grafeld Long's** poetry has appeared in *The Carolina Quarterly, Poet Lore, Journal of the American Medical Association* (JAMA) and other publications. She lives with her family in Arlington, where she teaches English at Marymount University. **George Looney's** first book, *Animals Housed in the Pleasure of Flesh*, won the 1995 Bluestem Award. His second book, *Attendant Ghosts*, will be published by Cleveland State University Press in the fall of 2000. He teaches creative writing at Penn State Erie, and serves as the translation editor for *Mid-American Review*. **Malinda Markham's** work has been published or is forthcoming in *Conjunctions, Paris Review, American Letters & Commentary, Ohio Review*, and others. **Michael McCole** is from Long Island and recently received an MA from Hollins College. This is his first published story. **Michael B. McMahon** teaches at Fresno Pacific University, a small Mennonite school in the San Joaquin Valley. His poems have appeared in such magazines as *Seneca Review, Green Mountains Review, Tar River Poetry, Poet Lore*, and *Hiram Poetry Review*. His translation of Jesus Serra's book of poems, *Páramos en la Memoria*, was published by the University of the Andes Press (Venezuela, 1994). **James McMichael's** most recent book is *The World at Large: New and Selected Poems, 1971-1996*. He teaches at the University of California, Irvine. **Christopher Merrill's** most recent books are *Only the Nails Remain: Scenes from the Balkan Wars* (nonfiction) and the translation of Aleš Debeljak's *The City and the Child*. He teaches at the College of the Holy Cross. **Carolyn Moran** is an assistant professor of English at Tennessee State University. Her work has appeared in *San Jose Studies, Xanadu, Cotton Boll/Atlanta Review, Puerto del Sol, Voices International, South Florida Poetry Review*, among other journals. She formerly taught at the University of Kansas, where she received a Helen and Jesse Jacobs Foundation Award for fiction and the Merrill and Edward M. Hopkins Awards for literary studies. **J. Morris** is a musician and writer living near Washington, D.C. He has published prose and poetry in many literary magazines in the U.S. and Great Britain, including *The Southern Review, Missouri Review, Prairie Schooner, The Formalist, Pleiades,* and *Five Points.* **Simone Muench** has work published in *River Oak Review, Crab Orchard Review, Many Mountains Moving, Glimmer Train's Poetry Presentation*, etc. She is the new poetry editor of *ACM* (Another Chicago Magazine) and recently received an Illinois Arts Council Award. **Paul Muldoon**, who was born in Northern Ireland in 1951, is the author of eight collections of poetry, most recently *Hay* and *The Annals of Chile*, which won the T.S. Eliot Prize in 1994. His *New Selected Poems 1968-94* won the 1997 Irish Times Prize for Poetry. Paul Muldoon is Howard G.B. Clark '21 Professor in the Humanities at Princeton University and Professor of Poetry at the University of Oxford. **Jere Odell** lives in South Bend, Indiana. His poems have appeared in *First Things, ACM,* and *Mudfish.* **Andrew Osborn** will soon complete his English dissertation, "Admit Impediments: The Use of Difficulty in Late-20th-Century American Poetry," at the University of Texas, Austin. His reviews and poems have recently appeared in *Boston Review, Iowa Review, Chicago Review, Poetry Project Newsletter, Colorado Review,* and *Fence.* An interview with August Kleinzahler and article on Paul Muldoon's fuzzy rhyme are forthcoming in *Verse* and *Contemporary Literature*, respectively. **Michael Perkins** is a poet, novelist and critic whose work has appeared widely. He is the author of *The Secret Record* (William Morrow and Company) and five collections of poetry, including *The Persistence of Desire* and *Gift of Choice.* **R.D. Skillings** has just published his fourth book of stories, *Where the Time Goes* (Univerity Press of New England). He has been associated with the Fine Arts Work Center in Provincetown since 1969. **Ken Smith** lives in London. He is the recipient of a Cholmondely Award and of a Lannan Award. His most recent book is *Wild Root* (Bloodaxe Books). **Laura-Gray Street** is a graduate of Hollins College (BA), the University of Virginia (MA) and the Warren Wilson Program for Writers (MFA). She teaches at Randolph-Macon Woman's College in Lynchburg, Virginia. Recent poems have appeared in *The Greensboro Review* and *The Louisville Review.* **Virgil Suarez** was born in Cuba in 1962. He is the author of over twelve books of fiction, prose, and poetry. His most recent is a collection of poems titled *In the Republic of Longing* published by Arizona State University's Bilingual Review Press. He is at work on a new novel. He teaches creative writing at Florida State University. **Maria Terrone**, the director of public relations for Hunter College of the City University of New York, has published in such magazines as *Poetry, Poet Lore, Atlantic Review, The Crab Orchard Review,* and *Wind,* which awarded her poem, "In Standard Time," the 1998 Allen Tate Memorial Poetry Prize. She has completed a full-length poetry manuscript, *The Bodies We Were Loaned.* **Ryan G. Van Cleave** is a freelance photographer originally from Chicago whose work has appeared in recent issues of *Oxford Magazine, Maryland Review, The Christian Science Monitor,* and *Poems & Plays;* new work is forthcoming in *Shenandoah, Quarterly West, Mid-American Review,* and *Southern Humanities Review.* He's the editor of *Sundog: The Southeast Review* and also serves as coordinator for the annual "World's Best Short Short Story" competition. His first book, *American Diaspora,* is forthcoming from the University of Iowa Press. **Martin Walls** was born in Brighton, England. A 1998 Winner of the "Discovery"/The Nation award, his work appears in *The Nation, Ohio Review, Five Points, Boulevard,* and *The Gettysburg Review* among others. His first book, *Small Human Detail in Care of National Trust,* will be published by New Issues Press in 2000. **Henry Weinfield's** new book of poems is entitled *The Sorrows of Eros and Other Poems* (University of Notre Dame Press, 1999). He is the author of a translation of and commentary on Stéphane Mallarmé's *Collected Poems* (University of California Press, 1995) and of a critical study, *The Poet Without a Name: Gray's Elegy and the Problem of History* (Southern Illlinois UP, 1991). He teaches at the University of Notre Dame. **Daniel Weissbort** directed the University of Iowa Translation Workshop for twenty-five years. He has now returned to his native England where he continues to edit the magazine *Modern Poetry In Translation* which he founded with the late Ted Hughes in 1965. His most recent collection of poetry is *What Was All The Fuss About?* (Anvil Press). **Terence Winch** is the author of *The Great Indoors* (Story Line, 1995), and *Irish Musicians/American Friends* (Coffee House, 1986), which received an American Book Award. His work has appeared in many magazines and anthologies, including the *1997 Best American Poetry.* He received an NEA poetry fellowship in 1992. **Wayne Zade** published, with Carolyn Perry, an interview with the essayist Scott Russell Sanders in the Winter 2000 issue of the *Kenyon Review.* He is currently working on a book of interviews of American jazz musicians on their experiences of playing and traveling in Japan.

# INDEX: ISSUES 1-9

Di Camillo, Kevin
    *Tonkinish; James Thomas Stevens – review –* ....................................................................... I,152
    *The Beautiful Monk* ......................................................................................................... VIII,137
    *Most Way Home – review –* ............................................................................................. VIII, 154
Dischell, Stuart
    *Evening V*
    *The Rockpile* ..................................................................................................................... II,39
Doerr, Joe Francis
    *The Only World; Lynda Hull – review –* .......................................................................... III,135
    *Woman Police Officer in Elevator; Lasdun James – review –* ............................................ IV, 147
    *Soulskin and Warscape with Lovers; Marilyn Krysl – review –* ........................................ V,152
    *An Interview with Ken Smith* ........................................................................................... VI,40
    *The Falling Hour; David Wojahn – review –* .................................................................. VI,145
D'Souza, Anthony
    *Dogfight and Other Stories – review –* ............................................................................. VII,145
    *A Blue Moon in Poorwater – review –* ............................................................................. IX,154
Dwenger, Randall
    *Symmetry* ......................................................................................................................... V,119
Eaton, Kathy
    *Stealing the Mona Lisa; Chris Greenhalgh – review –* ..................................................... II,125
Elman, Richard
    *Namedropping* .................................................................................................................. I,128
    *As Always, "Uncle Barney"* ............................................................................................. II,20
    *The Poverty of Rutubeuf* ................................................................................................... VI,4
Engels, John
    *Heron*
    *The Orders* ....................................................................................................................... VIII,34
Fagan, Kathy
    *Cinéma Vérité* .................................................................................................................. III,23
Faivre, Rob
    *Walking (excerpts)* ........................................................................................................... VIII,68
Falco, Edward
    *Therapy* ............................................................................................................................ II,113
    *Interviewed by Julia Cosmides* ........................................................................................ III, 33
    *Ghosts* .............................................................................................................................. VIII,38
Fennelly, Beth Ann
    *The Insecurities of Great Men* .......................................................................................... III,111
    *Windows of Prague*
    *Easter in the Beskydy Mountains* ..................................................................................... IV,28
Finch, Annie
    *A Letter for Emily Dickinson*
    *A Poulenc Hour* ............................................................................................................... IX,30
Finkelstein, Norman
    *Scribe* ............................................................................................................................... IX,32
Finnegan, James
    *Dirigible Days*
    *Purple* .............................................................................................................................. IX,60
Galindo, Esteban I.V.
    *Face of an Angel; Denise Chavez – review –* .................................................................... II,126
Gardner, Geoffrey
    *Welcome*
    *Inland in this World* ......................................................................................................... IX,54
Gibbons, Reginald
    *Sparrow* ........................................................................................................................... III,46
Gibson, Stephen
    *Belief* ............................................................................................................................... V,104
Gies, Martha
    *October Song* ................................................................................................................... VI,72
    *Plaintiff* ........................................................................................................................... VII,111
Gold, Elizabeth
    *Brown Recluse* ................................................................................................................. V,102
Goldensohn, Barry
    *The Death of Seneca*
    *Richard II* ........................................................................................................................ IV,33
Goldensohn, Lorrie
    *Semiotics*
    *Skid* ................................................................................................................................. V,44

# SUSTAINERS

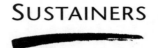

*Kevin DiCamillo*

*Gary & Elizabeth Gutchess*

*John F. Hayward*

*Samuel Hazo*

*Tim Kilroy*

*Richard Landry*

*Steve Lazar*

*Carol A. Losi*

*Jessica Maich*

*Vincent J. O'Brien*

*Daniel O'Donnell*

*Beth Haverkamp Powers*

*Kenneth L. Woodword*

Sustainers are lifetime subscribers to the *Notre Dame Review*. You can become a sustainer by making a one-time donation of $250 or more. (See subscription information enclosed.)

# Winner of the 2000 Richard Sullivan Prize in Short Fiction

## REVENGE OF UNDERWATER MAN AND OTHER STORIES

Jarda Cervenka

Jarda Cervenka

Revenge of Underwater Man

"In these magical tales, Jarda Cervenka moves with remarkable authority over the surface of the globe, from post-Cold War Prague to a remote Inuit village in Canada, from the dim light of a Japanese monastery to a Brussels brothel, and to ever more exotic realms—including memory itself, that most mysterious kingdom. This is the book of an adventurer, and the voice of these wry knowing stories remains as arresting as the keen eye taking in the wide world of oddity and appetite that binds them together. The stories here are lyric and tough-minded, and everywhere display the best quality of fiction, each story unfolding almost off-handedly, but finally, with captivating inevitability." —**Patricia Hampl**, author of *A Romantic Education, Virgin Times, Spill Will* and *I Could Tell You Stories*

0-268-04000-1 • $25.00 cloth//0-268-04001-X • $16.00 paper

# 1998 Richard Sullivan Prize winner

## IN THE HOUSE OF BLUE LIGHTS

Susan Neville

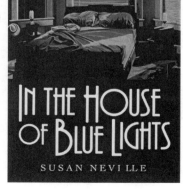

1998 WINNER OF THE RICHARD SULLIVAN PRIZE IN SHORT STORIES

IN THE HOUSE OF BLUE LIGHTS

SUSAN NEVILLE

"Troubled relationships among everyday people take center stage in this heart-wrenching short-story collection set in the Midwest."
—*Chicago Tribune*

0-268-01184-2 • $14.00 paper

Available at bookstores, or order from:
UNIVERSITY OF NOTRE DAME PRESS
Chicago Distribution Center
11030 South Langley Avenue
Chicago, IL 60628
Tel: 773-568-1550
http://www.undpress.nd.edu

# CAMPAIGN AMERICA '96

The View from the Couch, Second Edition

*With a New Epilogue: "From Monica to Milosevic, 1998-1999"*

William O'Rourke

"An engaging, nicely exasperated account of the 1996 campaign for the presidency . . . Some of the set pieces here, including his dissection of Dole's and Clinton's convention speeches, are hilarious, and his portrait of the obsessive shallowness of the media is convincing and alarming. A highly unusual contribution to the study of politics and media." —*Kirkus Reviews*

"P. J. might be the royalist O'Rourke, but William is the populist O'Rourke and he is easily twice as perceptive and funny. Anyone interested in campaign 2000 will need to read this book." —David Black, author of *King of Fifth Avenue* and *Murder at the Met*

Available at bookstores, or order from:

**UNIVERSITY OF NOTRE DAME PRESS**

Chicago Distribution Center
11030 South Langley Avenue
Chicago, IL 60628
Tel: 773-568-1550

http://www.undpress.nd.edu

0-268-02251-8 • $20.00 paper